# Dudley Girls High School
*A portrait of a school 1881-1975*

# Dudley Girls High School
*A portrait of a school 1881-1975*

First edition published by The Robinswood Press on behalf of the MB Ambrose Memorial Fund 2002.

© 2002 Maureen DuMont, Hilary Edwards, Barbara Evans, Beryl Fisher, Joan Hawes, Margaret Hiscox, Norma Homer, Pamela Hunt.

The above have asserted their rights under the Copyright, Designs and Patents Act 1988 to be identified as the authors of this work.

Design and layout by Steve Emms. Cover design by Lorraine Payne.
Printed by Latimer Trend, Plymouth.

All rights reserved. No part of this publication may be reproduced, stored in a retrieval system or transmitted in any form, or by any means, electronic, mechanical, photocopying, recording or otherwise, without the prior permission in writing from the publisher.

The Robinswood Press

Stourbridge  England

ISBN 1-869981-74X

# Contents

| | | |
|---|---|---|
| | Foreword | 5 |
| | Acknowledgements | 6 |
| | Preface | 7 |
| Section 1 | In the Beginning 1881-1914 | 9 |
| Section 2 | A New Era 1914-1919 | 27 |
| Section 3 | Between the Wars 1920-1939 | 37 |
| Section 4 | Wartime 1939-1945 | 67 |
| Section 5 | Post-War Era 1945-1960 | 83 |
| Section 6 | The Sixties | 103 |
| Section 7 | The Seventies | 119 |
| Section 8 | The End of the High School | 125 |
| Section 9 | School Uniform | 135 |
| Section 10 | Careers A-Z | 141 |

*Dedicated to Miss Ambrose*

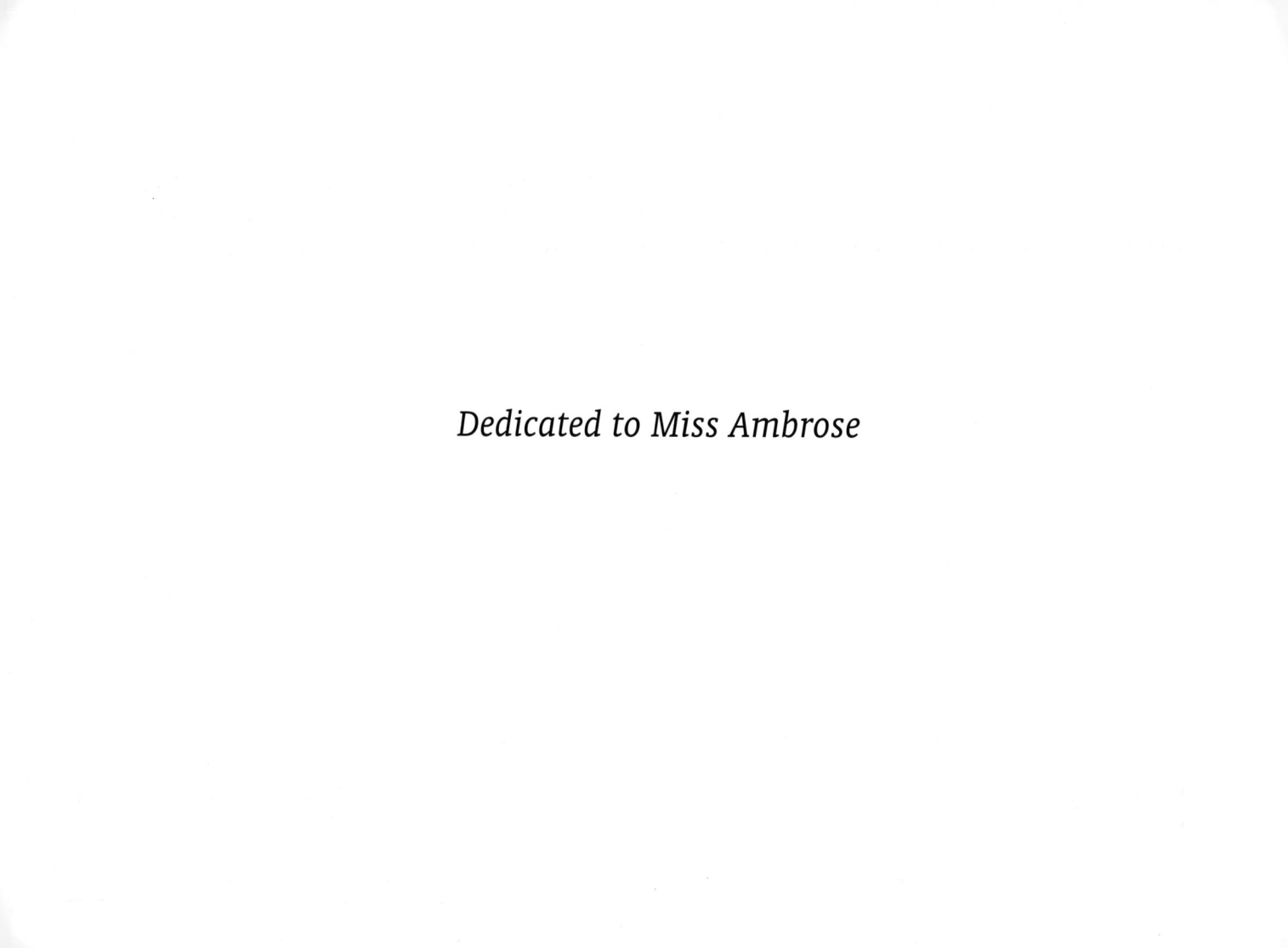

# Foreword

You leave school but school never leaves you. Wherever you end up in life you remember the things you did, the teachers who taught you and your classmates – both friends and enemies. The one great comfort of being a teacher, I've always thought, is that although they probably forget most of the pupils they herd towards the outside world, most members of the herd never forget them. And this member of the herd has certainly never forgotten Miss Ambrose.

It's only right and proper (at least it *was* in the middle of the last century) that you should be in awe of your head teacher and we were all in awe of Miss Ambrose. But her stern demeanour belied a care and understanding for and of her pupils which, from this distance, one appreciates in a way one couldn't at the time. Her requirements that we girls be diligent and reliable while ambitious and independent of mind has resonated through my life.

My seven years at DGHS gave me an indispensable grounding for what came after. It was the epitome of what my generation called *'a grammar school education'* – strong, detailed, wide-ranging, paying great attention to all aspects of the curriculum to ensure we left the school well versed in all the essential subjects – which included in those days some of the subjects considered non-essential today: music, sport, public speaking and drama.

Looking back I realise that I learned more at my school, Dudley Girls' High School, than I have learned anywhere else and I shall always remain in its debt for that.

Sue Lawley
Summer 2002

# Acknowledgements

Thanks are due to the group of former staff and pupils, Maureen DuMont, Hilary Edwards, Barbara Evans, Beryl Fisher, Joan Hawes, Margaret Hiscox, Norma Homer and Pamela Hunt, for the inspiration, drive, co-ordination – and most of the writing – which ensured the completion of the project.

Special thanks are due to Gwen Jennings, for the cover paintings and illustrations of the School uniforms; to Sue Lawley, for the Foreword; and to Jenny Wilkes and BBC Pebble Mill for their broadcast which resulted in even more contacts.

Thanks also to so many individuals and institutions who provided information, archive material, old copies of *The Cornflower*, photographs, donations, written contributions – and for those who underwent such intensive interviewing for a myriad of historical data! These are too numerous to include in detail, but special mention must be made of Dudley Archives Department, Dudley Women's Development Fund, David Humphries, Dorothy Turley, the family of Dorothy Round, the Staff of Dudley Library and Information Centre, the Staff at Castle High School, especially Val Parker, and Chris Marshall and Steve Emms for guidance on publication. In addition, to copyright holders, particularly the *Express and Star*, for permission to use photographic material – and to those that we have been unable to trace.

By no means last, thanks also to the husbands of some of the authors, for their tireless patience and support.

# Preface

Dudley Girls' High School no longer exists – either as a building or as a School in its own right. During its long history, however, it influenced the lives of many throughout the Dudley area.

In October 1999, a small group of former staff and pupils felt inspired to write the story of the School. When, a few months later, the former Headmistress, Miss Ambrose, died it was decided that this story would be dedicated to her. A fund was later established, following her Memorial Service, to finance the production of a book.

This book is the result of the efforts of that group – and of the many individuals and institutions who supported the project with information and anecdotes, photographs and illustrations, and advice, funding and enthusiasm. It cannot tell the story of everything and everyone in its past. But it does give those who read it a flavour of its history and how its pupils were educated.

## Section One

# In the Beginning 1881-1914

DURING THE SECOND HALF of the nineteenth century a great enthusiasm for secondary education arose. The Education Act of 1870 had made elementary education compulsory, but there was no public provision for secondary schools. So secondary education was available only to the children of parents who could afford to pay fees at Public, Endowed or Private Schools.

In November 1880, a group of prominent Dudley businessmen met to discuss the possibility of setting up a school for their daughters – Dudley Grammar School for Boys had been founded in 1562. At this meeting, the Dudley Proprietary School for Girls was established. It was set up as a Limited Company with £5 shares, each share entitling one girl to attend the School which was to be modelled on Edgbaston High School for Girls. This, in turn, had been based on Miss Buss's renowned North London Collegiate School. Premises were purchased at the corner of Wolverhampton Street and Trinity Road in Dudley, and the School opened on 28th April 1881 with 24 girls, whose ages ranged from 7 to 14 years.

The first Headmistress was Miss Moss (1881-1883), sister of Dr Moss, the headmaster of Shrewsbury School. One of the first pupils of the School gives a picture of her new Headmistress. Writing in the School magazine, *The Cornflower*, in 1931, Miss Watson recalls:

"*To one like myself, who was rather a small girl, Miss Moss seemed a most imposing personality, especially when she came into our classroom to take prayers. Then she was arrayed, or so it seemed to my childish mind, in something in the nature of a scarlet robe with fancy trimmings all down the front (or was it a red dressing gown?) and, dare I say it, wearing soft carpet slippers. Her hair was elaborately done up in the then fashionable 'chignon'. We were all very fond of her.*"

An early School photograph

Miss Moss was succeeded as Headmistress by Miss Green, who had been on the staff of Edgbaston High School. Miss Green (1883-1891) first came to Dudley when the School was still in Wolverhampton Street. Aged only 28, she was afraid that the members of the Council might consider her too young for the post. So she borrowed a bonnet, veil and cape and presented herself so well that her age never came into question.

Miss Green remained in Dudley until 1891 when she left to take up a similar post in Constantinople. She finally retired some years before the Great War. When hostilities broke out, as she spoke eight languages, she offered her services to the French Government and trained as a French army nurse. After the War she lived for a time in the South of France and then in Paris. She often returned to Dudley and talked of her adventures.

**Miss Green**

Meanwhile, the School itself soon built up such a good reputation that places were in great demand. Larger premises were acquired in St James's Road to accommodate the increasing number of pupils:

*"The building was Scholastic English Gothic of the 15th Century type, with a bold tracery window in the large hall. On the ground floor it contained a reception room and three large lofty classrooms. On the first floor, approached by a wide stone staircase, was a large assembly hall with open-timbered pitch pine roof and large stone tracery windows at either end, and class- and music-rooms adjoining. There was also a cloak room, a lavatory and a drying cabinet in the basement. The classrooms were heated by open-fire ventilating stoves, and the large hall, cloakroom and corridor by hot water."*

Front of St James's Road School

Blocksidge's Almanac of 1885 shows that admissions to the School were by shareholder nomination, each share carrying one nomination. A similar publication in 1887 describes the School curriculum:

> *The course of instruction is most comprehensive, including French, German, Latin, Natural Science and Class Singing, Music being the only subject charged as an extra. The fees were graduated according to age and commenced for girls under 10 at four-and-a-half guineas per annum. The College of Preceptors and the Cambridge Local Examination Board held examinations. The whole School was examined annually by an independent examiner whose report was published.*

1891 saw the arrival of Miss M E Burke (1891-1914) as Miss Green's successor. She was the first and only graduate on the staff, having gained a BA at London University. Women graduates were rare in

**Lecture Room with tracery window**

**Tennis court at rear of School**

those days! She taught almost every subject of the curriculum in the upper forms, in addition to her exacting duties as Headmistress. She was a good teacher, but it is rather as Headmistress that she is remembered. Her patience, her understanding of girls whose temperaments and outlook were utterly unlike her own, her ever-ready sympathy, her utter unworldliness, her humility and unselfishness made her a living example to the girls who regarded her with great affection and reverence.

On one hot day in June, Miss Burke took a party of girls for a tennis match to a school in the neighbourhood. The tea table was decorated with bowls of flowers called coreopsis, which have bright yellow petals and a brown centre. Miss Burke and the girls were told that, as it matched their School colours, they had adopted the coreopsis as their 'school flower'.

**Miss Burke**

The Dudley girls thought this was a brilliant idea and immediately wanted a flower to be adopted by Dudley High School. Various flowers were suggested. After much discussion among the Staff and girls, the matter was voted upon, but then it was found that the 'pink' – also known as dianthus – and the cornflower had tied. Finally, however, it was decided to nominate the cornflower because it matched the School colour, blue, so well. It was also easy to obtain! From then on, the cornflower was adopted as the School flower and gave its name to the School Magazine.

By 1896 the School's popularity had grown so much that a vital new extension was built. Opened in 1897 by Sir Gilbert Claughton, the new buildings included a Kindergarten classroom, a Form Room and a Dining Room. This extension enabled the school to offer a Kindergarten for both girls and boys – who were admitted up until 1944. There were 98 children in the School by 1889 and in 1903 the number had grown to 103 – compared to just 55 boys attending the Grammar School.

The Kindergarten department itself started in 1897 in the new School buildings in St James's Road and it became firmly established as an integral part of the later Priory Road school. By the 1920's there were three sections – the Preparatory, where boys and girls entered at four or five years old, the Lower School and the Junior School. Boys left at the age of eight. Interestingly, Miss Frood, the then Headmistress, had a policy that girls in the Kindergarten should not be awarded prizes for work, as 'doing well' was enough. The boys, however, were rewarded!

**Early form photograph – about 1892**

**Early production – about 1897**

Their classrooms were NE, NI, the Annexe and the Handwork Room which gave easy access to the garden and pond. The pond was a great attraction and when children were missing it was the obvious place to look for them. Gardening was an important part of the Kindergarten timetable. Each class had a patch which was situated at the far side of the quadrangle.

Jean Buckingham remembers the halfpenny paid for a small bar of Cadbury's chocolate and one-third-of-a-pint of milk. Only half of the chocolate was to be eaten, the remainder taken home for mother. Joyce Round recalls Mrs Bradney handing out Horlicks tablets which replaced the chocolate. After lunch, the youngest children – in the Preparatory Class – were encouraged to rest on little camp beds.

**Miss Plant and Kindergarten pupils 1931**

**Staff circa 1887**

# Dudley Municipal High School for Girls

(Established 1881),

AND

# Kindergarten for Boys and Girls.

### STAFF.

Head Mistress  -  Miss BURKE, B.A. (Lond.)

Assistant Mistresses :—

MISS TRINDER, Cambridge Higher Local Examination and Cambridge Teachers' Diploma.

MISS HOLLINSHEAD, London Matriculation. 1st Class in Mathematics (South Kensington).

MISS WOODHOUSE, Higher Certificate of the Frœbel Society. Drawing and Physiology (South Kensington).

MISS PEARCE, L.L.A. (St. Andrew's)    MISS LEWIS.

### VISITING TEACHERS.

French :         MADAMOISELLE BOISOT.

Pianoforte :     MISS F. SCOTT, Leipzig Conservatorium.

Pianoforte :     MISS E. DEERING { Higher Certificate of the Associated Board of the R.A.M. and R.C.M.

Violin :         MR. MORTIMER REIDY, L.R.A.M.

Singing :        MR. WEAVER STEPHENS, Graduate of the Tonic Sol Fa College.

Swedish Drill and Gymnastics : MISS L. R. TAYLOR, Dartford Physical Training College.

Drawing : { MR. D. JONES, Headmaster of the School of Art, A.R.C.A.
           { MR. J. W. ASH, Second Master of the School of Art.

Physics and Chemistry : MR. F. E. THOMPSON, A.R.C.S., F.C.S.

---

The School was opened in 1881, by private enterprise, in order to give a thoroughly efficient education of High School Standard at a moderate cost, and has since been purchased by the Dudley Education Committee. It is situated in one of the pleasantest parts of the town, within ten minutes' walk of the London and North-Western and Great Western Railway Stations. It is built with every modern convenience and includes a large Hall, six Class Rooms, Music Rooms, Kindergarten Room, and Dining Room. For Pupils residing at a distance dinner is provided.

The School maintains a high Standard of work, and the Pupils enter for various Public Examinations, including the Oxford Local Examinations, and those of the Associated Board of the Royal Academy of Music and Royal College of Music, the Tonic Sol Fa College and the Royal Drawing Society.

Careful attention is paid to the Physical Training of the Pupils; the drilling and gymnastic lessons form a regular part of the School work, and the Play Ground and Tennis Court give ample opportunity for outdoor exercise. The average number of Pupils in attendance during the last ten years is over 100.

### Subjects of Instruction.

| | |
|---|---|
| Scripture History | Geometry |
| English Literature | Botany |
| Grammar and Composition | Physiography (including Elementary Physics and Chemistry) |
| History | |
| Geography | Drawing (Freehand and Model) |
| French | Gymnastics |
| Latin | Class Singing |
| Arithmetic | Needlework |
| Algebra | |

Pupils are required to take such subjects of the above course of study as the Headmistress may consider advisable, due regard being paid to the health and age of the Pupils.

The work is inspected and tested periodically by examiners unconnected with the School.

Reports of Conduct and Progress are sent to the parents at the end of each term.

Girls who have completed their School course can be trained as Student Teachers, and prepared for the Examinations of the Frœbel Society or for other Examinations by special arrangement.

A Scholarship tenable for two years is awarded annually on the Work and Examinations of the highest Form. No Pupils can compete for this who have been less than two years in the School.

### School Hours.

| | | |
|---|---|---|
| Upper School | - | 9.10 to 12.45 and 2.20 to 4.20 |
| Lower School | - | 9.10 to 12.45 and 2.20 to 4 |
| Preparatory Class | - | 9.30 to 12.30 (afternoon optional) |
| Kindergarten Classes | - | 9.30 to 12.30 |

The School year is divided into three terms of about 13 weeks each.

### Fees.

#### School Fees.

| | | | | |
|---|---|---|---|---|
| Pupils under 5 years | .... | £1 1 0 | per term |
| ,, between 5 and 7 years | .... | 1 11 6 | ,, ,, |
| ,, ,, 7 ,, 11 ,, | .... | 2 2 0 | ,, ,, |
| ,, ,, 11 ,, 14 ,, | .... | 3 3 0 | ,, ,, |
| ,, over 14 years | .... | 4 4 0 | ,, ,, |

**N.B.**—*When Girls enter the School under the age of 6 years their fees do not rise above £3 3 0 during the School course.*

#### Extra Fees (Optional Subjects).

| | | |
|---|---|---|
| Pianoforte or Violin | £1 11 6 | per Term of 10 Lessons |
| Harmony .... | 0 10 6 | ,, ,, |
| Theory of Music .... | 0 5 0 | ,, ,, |
| Dancing .... | 1 1 0 | ,, ,, |

Girls not attending the School may take special subjects on payment of an extra fee for each subject.

All fees are due in advance on the first day of each term.

### Rules and Regulations.

1. A certificate of conduct is required in the case of girls over 9 years of age, coming from another School, signed by the Head Teacher of such School. The Committee reserve to themselves the right to request the withdrawal of any Pupil exercising a bad influence in the School, or who, through idleness or irregular attendance, does not make fair progress in her work.

2. No excuses can be taken for unprepared Lessons, except in cases of illness. In such cases, or in cases of unavoidable absence, a note signed by a parent or guardian must be brought stating the reason.

3. The Health Declaration Form, duly filled up and signed, must be brought on the first day of each term. No Pupil suffering from, or having been in contact with any infectious disease, is allowed to attend the School until a certificate of safety, signed by a Medical Practitioner, has been received by the Headmistress.

4. Should a Pupil's absence extend beyond three days, a note to explain the cause should be sent by post.

5. No Pupil may enter the School before 9.0 and 2.10, or remain after 1.0 and 4.30 without permission.

6. Dinner is provided at a charge of 8d. Pupils bringing lunch instead are charged 1d. as table money. Parents are particularly requested not to give permission to any girl to lunch in any shop or restaurant in the town.

7. Everything brought into School, including waterproof, boots and umbrella, must be clearly marked with the name of the owner.

8. Every pupil must be provided with shoes to change having *flat heels*, and with a bag in which to keep them, also a separate bag containing brush, comb and button hook if required. Pinafores or Aprons must be worn in School by the younger children, and by all forms at needlework lessons, and in the laboratory. A uniform dress is worn for gymnastics. Information as to material and pattern should be obtained from the Headmistress.

9. Notice of the withdrawal of any Pupil, or the discontinuance of an optional subject, must be given to the Headmistress in writing, at least six weeks before the end of a term, otherwise half a term's fees will be charged.

10. If, in consequence of illness or other sufficient cause approved by the Headmistress, a Pupil shall have been absent the whole of the term, or has not made more than twenty attendances, the fees are carried forward to her credit for the following term; but no allowance can be made if more than twenty attendances have been made during the term.

11. The Headmistress may be seen at the School on Wednesdays in term time between 2.30 and 4.30, or by appointment.

As rumours of change in Education began to circulate in 1943 the future of the Kindergarten came into question. The 1944 Education Act brought in 'Scholarship-only places' for the School – the girls could no longer move up automatically from the Junior School. The Act, though, sounded the death knell for the Kindergarten and from then on numbers steadily declined. In 1945, Miss Clifford wrote:

> *It is hard to visualise the School without 'the little ones' but we have to face the fact that within two or three years we shall be a school without a Kindergarten.*

By 1948, the few girls remaining, who hoped to pass the Scholarship, were taught in the Annexe by Miss Nock but the following year the Kindergarten came to an end.

Back in the 1890's, however, both Kindergarten and main School were flourishing and developing. In 1904, the Corporation of Dudley acquired the School as a 'going concern' from the Governors and maintained it until 1910 as The Dudley Municipal High School.

Dudley was, at that time, a fast-growing town and further expansion was needed to cope with an ever-increasing demand for places at the Municipal High School. The St James's Road site had no room for any further expansion and a new, larger location was therefore needed. So began the plans for the Priory Road building.

Since 1890 there had been a 'Pupil-Teacher Centre' located in the Old Technical School in Stafford Street for Dudley and Staffordshire girls, but the days of the 'Pupil-Teacher' were over. The two authorities jointly resolved to provide a new modern school with an ambitious curriculum, housed in the finest building that could be designed, for the girls from the 'Pupil-Teacher Centre' and the Municipal High School. All came together, at last, to form the Dudley Girls' High School (DGHS).

The Honourable Mrs John Ward laid the Foundation Stone for the building on 16th September 1909. Millicent and Hilda Foley remember the move to the new building in Priory Road in 1910:

*"Do you remember the great trek from the Old School to the New? Solemnly in the Hall that morning the order had gone forth that at long last the Great Move was to be made. Each girl was to carry her satchel of books, and bags containing shoes, brush and comb. Everything must be carried through with due order and*

Laying the Foundation Stone

Staffs. County & Dudley County Borough Councils

**DUDLEY GIRLS' HIGH SCHOOL.**

**CEREMONY**

OF

**LAYING THE FOUNDATION STONE,**

ON

Thursday, 16th September, 1909,

BY

**The Honourable Mrs. John H. Ward.**

Programme for laying foundation stone, Dudley Girls' High School, 1909

Order of proceedings

decorum. And so, wearing our hard-brimmed sailor hats, our coats buttoned to the bottom lest any knee might show, and neatly gloved, we sallied forth. In a long crocodile, each mistress striding ahead of her form, in solemn procession we marched into our new 'Alma Mater'. Do you remember the fun we made of the Italians still at work on our arrival? Do you remember being reported by a prefect and suitably punished for walking arm-in-arm with your school chum or being denied games for several weeks for lolling in an 'unladylike' position while watching a Company Netball match? Do you remember receiving an 'order mark' as a punishment for being seen in the road without gloves, or walking in puddles all the way to school so that you might spend the afternoon in the drying-room drying your socks? Do you remember wearing a red satin bow on your shoulder for being top of the form for that week?"

Three sisters, M G, E M and M H Osborn recall:

"We walked about School in single file and in deadly silence, and for breaches of these rules received order marks. Then we had weekly places in class, which were read out on Monday morning at prayers, regardless of the mixed feelings of all concerned. The School was divided into companies and each strove to win honours for itself. We also had prize distributions, when we all wore white dresses and white hair ribbons."

The official opening of the new buildings took place on Thursday, 8th December 1910.

In his Opening Ceremony speech, as reported by 'The Herald', the Honourable Whitelaw Reid set the tone for the new School:

"I am glad that this is a girls' school. The old idea that those who kept the home and reared the future generation did not really need as much elementary education as their comrades who merely brought in the supplies was the notion of a barbarous age. I am glad that it is a school for secondary education of

**Dudley Girls' High School circa 1910**

**Staffordshire County Council**
and
**Dudley County Borough**
EDUCATION COMMITTEES.

## Dudley Girls' High School.

OFFICIAL
**OPENING OF NEW BUILDINGS**
in
PRIORY ROAD, DUDLEY,
Thursday, December 8th, 1910.
at 3 p.m.
BY HIS EXCELLENCY
THE AMERICAN AMBASSADOR
(THE HON. WHITELAW REID).

**Programme** of **Proceedings.**

Outside of programme

girls. The world outgrew those who, entrusted with the high duties of their sex, really needed only to know how to read, write and cipher and how to bake and sew, even if the circumstances permitted them to go further. Certainly those are admirable features of education – all as admirable as the alphabet and multiplication tables. But when boys have time for more so surely their sisters have – and if so, it is not merely a blunder but a crime to keep them back from the facilities for secondary education as good as their brothers enjoy."

Amongst the earliest appointments in 1910 were Mr and Mrs Jeffries, the first caretakers of the superb new buildings – who stayed in charge of them for 23 years. Miss Frood later recorded their efforts in *The Cornflower*:

"Mr and Mrs Jeffries have been part of the School for so long that it is difficult to think of DGHS without them. Many will remember Mrs Jeffries for her excellent school dinners, her teas and suppers at School functions, and for her many acts of kindness, especially to harassed members of staff at the end of term or during School plays. The School kitchen was a marvel of tidiness and many remarked on the high standards of cleanliness for the whole building. Mrs Jeffries has a perfect genius for finding lost tennis balls with the help of Gyp, the dog. Mr Jeffries will be long remembered for his ever-ready and invaluable help in the production of School plays. No task was too difficult for him. He was a skilled carpenter, electrician and gardener. The South Border is the admiration of all who pass by the School. Mr Jeffries enjoyed teaching carpentry to the boys. Mr and Mrs Jeffries both had a delightful sense of humour. No school could have had more devoted and loyal friends."

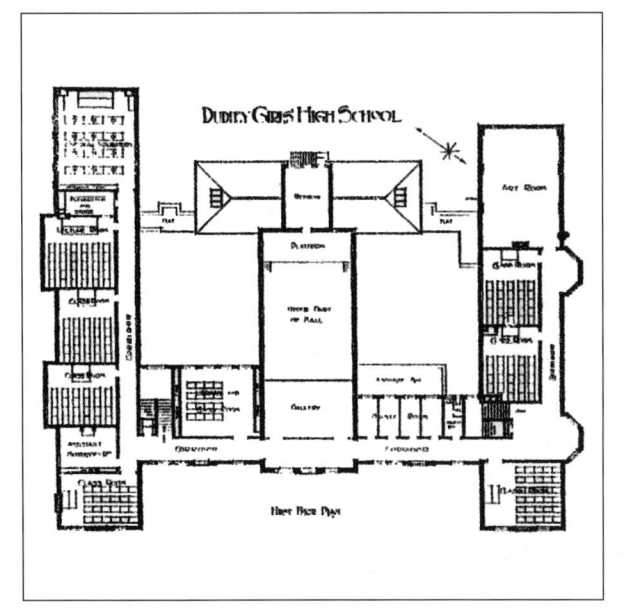

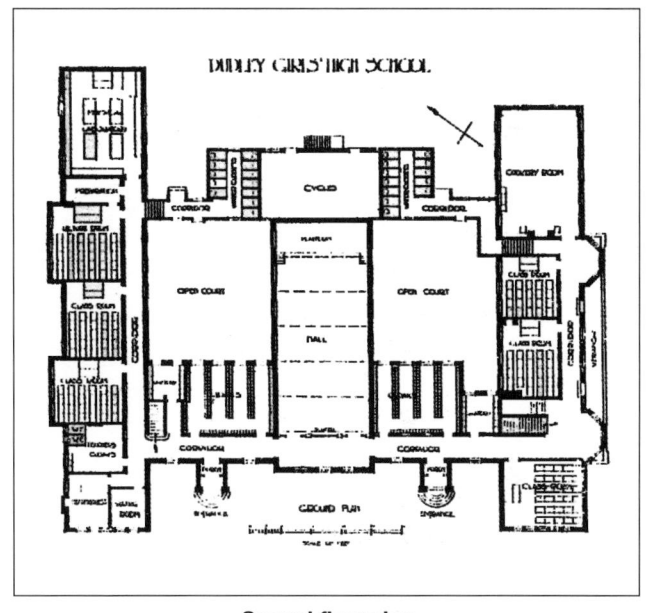

**First floor plan**

**Ground floor plan**

**Mr and Mrs Jeffries
1910-1933**

In its new surroundings, with more facilities and more space, the School grew and changed rapidly. Miss Burke was proud of 'her child', as she felt the School to be, proud of its growth and delighted when increased numbers made possible the appointment of a highly qualified Staff.

However, Miss Burke loved 'people' rather than 'organisations', and 'smaller groups' rather than 'large assemblies'. It was therefore with some relief – yet tinged with regret – that she handed over the reins of government in 1914 to a younger successor in whose powers she had full confidence and whose friendship she greatly valued in later years.

With the coming of Miss Frood, a new era in the history of the School began.

**The Staff 1913**

## Section Two

# A New Era 1914-1919

MISS FROOD arrived at the beginning of World War I to a School of sailor-hatted girls, with the intention of staying for three years. But she became so fascinated by the town and its High School that she remained as Headmistress in Dudley for the next 27 years. Miss Frood (1914-1941) had a new vision. She didn't conform to the generally accepted standards of a Head. She had a flair for clothes. She had chic hats and – what is more – knew how to wear them! It was soon realised that she had what then seemed to be unconventional ideas on the subject of school administration generally and the part that the girls themselves should take in shaping the internal life of the School. Her aim of giving freedom through self-government and encouraging girls to make School Rules was revolutionary. *"Rules forced upon a man from without are made to be broken."*

Her work in Dudley became recognised in the wider educational world as she made DGHS into one of the best day schools in the country. Great interest was also shown in the School's Art owing to Miss Frood's passion for the subject. Art was alive and pervaded the whole of school life. *'Dudley children see beauty in the Black Country'* was the press heading when the School's paintings were exhibited in London.

Miss Frood's accounts of foreign visits – particularly to Russia – inspired her pupils. In 1924 a School party visited Paris and exchange holidays with French girls followed. Her work for the League of Nations was such that money was collected for the Save the Children Fund and an orphaned European child was 'adopted'.

No one could fail to realise the intense vitality and vivid personality which Miss Frood possessed. Her enthusiasm, which swept all obstacles before her, and her whole-hearted interest in everything related to her work enabled her to carry the School from strength to strength. Stupendous tasks –

such as raising more than £1000 for a Scholarship and Loan Fund, which had seemed well-nigh impossible, were accomplished successfully after the dynamic call of *"Let's do it"* from Miss Frood.

In 1939, to celebrate her Silver Jubilee as Head of the School, the Old Girls presented her with a cheque. She planned to use this for the making of a rose garden where the flowers would remind her of the girls. She retired in 1941. Her successor, Miss Ambrose, felt privileged to succeed her, realising that Miss Frood had left behind a School that was, like herself, intensely alive. She died in 1954 and, on 23rd June 1955, her memorial garden was formally handed over to the School. Most of the beds were planted with roses.

**Miss Frood**

Although 1914 brought the positive leadership of Miss Frood, it also signalled the many problems of Wartime:

*"From time to time, we lined the corridors for Zeppelin drill when we heard the noise of the rattle. Of course, we never knew, when the alarm went, whether it was only a practice or the real thing. We spent every spare minute knitting, sewing and making parcels for the soldiers, and we collected for war funds."*

Fund-raising occupied much of the girls' time and included a two-day Sale of Work, and Concerts. Similarly, the growing of vegetables in the School grounds became an important part of the School's war effort:

*"In the Spring of 1917 it was decided to dig up the grass near the botany gardens and plant potatoes. Staff and girls alike did Trojan work in converting the area into a ploughed field. Oh, the rubbish that was*

brought to light! Large pieces of drain-pipes, bricks, stones, and terrible weeds were found everywhere. One particular root of bindweed was nicknamed 'Grandma' and extended the length of three gardens.

A few pessimists were sure potatoes would never grow in such hard, stony ground, but happily they turned out to be wrong, for our labours were rewarded by quite a respectable crop which was sold to the School for school dinners. Beans, peas, carrots, parsnips, beet and our old favourites, lettuces and radishes, were sown in the other parts of the gardens, and most of them did splendidly – especially the carrots. Altogether we spent about eight shillings on seeds, potatoes included, and we realised £2 7s 8d for the War Fund by the sale of vegetables so that the work was well worth doing."

---

DUDLEY GIRLS' HIGH SCHOOL

# Entertainment & Sale of Work

IN AID OF

THE DUDLEY CENTRAL WAR FUND.

*Friday and Saturday, Dec. 15th and 16th, 1916.*

PROGRAMME.   PRICE TWO-PENCE.

---

PART II.—5 to 6.

Friday and Saturday.  5.  "TO-MORROW."

CAST *in order of appearance.*

To-Morrow—M. Percy.  Dick—R. Rogers.  To-Night—W. Chatwin.
Day Hours—O. Jones, J. Baker, M. Wood, D. Benton, M. Turton, R. Walker, R. Perry, H. Penney, B. Smith, L. Marsh, M. Freakley, I. Morgan.
Night Hours—M. Norton, M. Osborns, I. Marsh, D. Coleman, I. Hartland, C. Cooksey, D. Barrow, E. Davies, M. Marsh, M. Lees, C. Pearce, A. Hughes.
St. Swithin—M. Hunt.  April Fool's Day—I. Speke.
Wet Day—M. Harley.  March 1st—D. D. Davies.
Fine Day—M. Grainger.  Dawn—F. L. Smith.
May Day—K. Fletcher.  To-Day—E. Aston.
St. Valentine's Day—M. Baker.  Year—H. Round.
New Year's Day—D. Shaw.  Red-Letter Days—M. Shaw, M. Beddowes.
Michaelmas—M. Taft.  Hallowe'en—K. Dews.
Christmas Day—M. Ball.  29th February, Leap Day—M. Plant.

ACT I. ... ... ... ... ... A glade in a wood.
ACT II. ... ... ... By the Sea: The Sands of time underfoot.
ACT III. ... ... ... The Hall of Feasting in the Palace of the Year.

6.—GOD SAVE THE KING.

Despite the pressures of war, the girls throughout the School were able to celebrate with Christmas parties. The Lower School party...

> ...commenced at 3 o'clock on 11th December. The majority of the girls wore party dresses and they looked so different from how they usually did. First we went into the Hall and played games. Then came tea, when buns, cakes and biscuits were handed round and then a cup of tea each. We talked and laughed and had a really good time. After tea we trooped back to the Hall and we had waltzing and Miss Frood came in. At last it came time to go home and all said that we'd had a good time.

And on the day of the Middle School party...

> ...we all wore our tunics and white blouses. I don't think there was a girl who was not looking forward to it. We brought our own tea, sugar and eatables. Miss Frood acted as

### BALANCE SHEET FOR YEAR 1917-1918

| RECEIPTS. | £ | s. | d. |
|---|---|---|---|
| Balance from previous year | 25 | 8 | 7½ |
| Sale of Postcards | 0 | 15 | 10 |
| Sale of Newspapers and Waste Paper | 3 | 11 | 3 |
| Sale of Vegetables | 2 | 17 | 6 |
| Sale of Embroidery | 1 | 6 | 6½ |
| Sale of Photographs | 0 | 12 | 6 |
| Proceeds of performance of "Playboy of the Western World" | 22 | 1 | 3 |
| Proceeds of School Sports | 16 | 14 | 9 |
| School Collections, etc. | 26 | 19 | 8 |
| Bank Interest | 0 | 11 | 0 |
| | £100 | 18 | 10¾ |

| EXPENDITURE. | £ | s. | d. |
|---|---|---|---|
| King George's Sailors' Fund | 6 | 0 | 8 |
| New Hospital Fund | 20 | 0 | 0 |
| G.P.U. Hut Fund | 15 | 0 | 0 |
| Dudley Hut Fund | 2 | 6 | 0 |
| Secondary Teachers' War Relief Fund | 22 | 1 | 3 |
| Dudley Central War Fund | 16 | 14 | 9 |
| Friends' Relief Fund | 10 | 10 | 0 |
| Balance | 8 | 6 | 2¾ |
| | £100 | 18 | 10¾ |

*hostess, shaking hands with every girl as she went in. The Hall and Dining Room were decorated with evergreens. First there was a polka and several other dances and games, which were great fun, and then tea-time came round. We all trooped into the Dining Room, which was lit by Chinese lanterns; the Upper School party committee waited on us. After tea there were more dances and games. The best game was 'Blindman's Buff'. 'Sir Roger de Coverley' was also much enjoyed, and we ended up by singing 'Auld Lang Syne'.*"

Whilst the Upper School party...

"*...was even more delightful than ever we had anticipated. The dancing was exciting for the Hall was so full that every two minutes you were bumping into someone. The games were also very enjoyable. 'Musical Bumps' and 'The Jolly Miller' were exciting and there was much laughter during the game of 'Darby and*

**Gardening**

**The Staff 1916**

Joan'. A 'Cautionary Song' by Miss Taylor and Miss Fenn was a great success and received an encore, and two scenes from 'Pickwick Papers' given by the Sixth Form evoked roars of laughter. We were very sorry when the party ended." – Innocent pleasure indeed!

At the Distribution of Certificates in December 1917, Lady Balfour was the Guest Speaker. Certificates were awarded, not for examination results, but for steady work during the year. In addressing the School, Lady Balfour said:

"Schools are like trees, they make the atmosphere healthy and they ought to be planted everywhere. How delightful it is to be trusted, as you in this School are. You have shut a door on a room containing rules and opened a door on a room containing principles. Principles are our guide through life. After the war there will be a majority of women in this country; that majority will make women important, they will help to decide the future of England. Education will help to decide rightly.

You learn a good many things at school, but it is not the things you learn so much as the way you are taught and the way you learn that matters. Professions that were closed to women before the war are now open to them and therefore their responsibility is the greater. I hope it will never be said that the girls of England hindered the men, or hindered their country. There is only one means by which we may become useful citizens – we must fear God and keep His commandments; we must remember our duty to our neighbour, for this is the whole duty of man."

The First World War ended in November 1918. *The Cornflower* of April 1919 records:

"*Praeterita. Praesentia. Futura.*
We have passed through an eventful year since the last issue of the Magazine; our motto seems peculiarly

*appropriate at this moment when all the world stands, as it were, in hesitation, looking back with relief to the past and forward with mingled feelings to the yet very uncertain future. Probably all present girls regretted that the five weeks' closing of the School during the influenza epidemic – which made a strange break in the School year – coincided with the conclusion of hostilities, so that we missed our corporate rejoicing."*

Miss Frood's vision of *'Democracy not Autocracy'* led to the most important event in 1919, the introduction of School and Form Courts. Dudley Girls' High School became renowned throughout the world for its self-government and welcomed many educationalists to see how it worked.

'Courts' were set up to provide a voice in the management of School affairs. Prior to this, order marks and every other form of punishment had been abolished. It was hoped that Courts would enable the School to become self-governing, introducing its own system of discipline and punishment. The Court of Honour met every other Thursday and the Form Courts alternate Tuesdays.

The Court of Honour included Staff, Prefects and Form Presidents above Lower Third. Matters which affected the whole School were discussed there. The Form President presided over the Form Courts with a Vice-President and Secretary – all elected by the members of each form. These Courts dealt with form matters – discipline, form activities, contests and competitions. The President reported the proceedings of the Court of Honour to the form.

It was hoped that, used in the right way and for the right things, the Courts would succeed in establishing a new style of freedom, democracy and responsibility. The reason for a special rule or regulation would not always be seen by all the girls, but it was hoped that, in time, they would all come to understand the 'whys and wherefores'. Hilda Head wrote an amusing version of the first meeting of the School Court in the 1919 issue of *The Cornflower*:

> *The Book of Law.*
> *Now it came to pass on the 16th day of January, 1919, that the Staff and divers members of the School thereof, repaired to the Art Room. And there was much laughter and excitement amongst the assembled congregation until a sudden silence fell upon them; and the President entered into the Court. And the word of the President came unto them saying, "This is the first meeting of the School Court, the object of which is to form and administer laws and to deal justly and wisely with all sinners, turning them into the paths of righteousness."*
>
> *And it came to pass that the congregation assembled as of yore. And when they were gathered the President arose and said – "Brethren, ye are called together to decide the momentous question of whether hair-slides shall be worn in School." And the Councillors waxed bold and preached and there was great dissension. For the children had worn clasps which had twinkled like myriads of stars of divers colours. Many had exhorted the children that they should refrain from these varieties, but the multitude was scarce restrained. Howbeit, a certain wise Councillor arose and consumed with fire one of these clasps. And great was the conflagration thereof.*
>
> *Then a great fear came upon the multitude, for by wearing these clasps their own tresses were in danger of burning by fire, wherefore the learned Council decided that these varieties should cease and that plain apparel should be worn. And so it was so and the appearance of the School was much improved thereby.*

## Section Three

# Between the Wars 1920-1939

WITH THE END of the First World War the School began to broaden its horizons. Links were made with a school in St Quentin, France, and girls corresponded with pen-friends there. This resulted in a trip to Paris in 1924, and several exchange visits between the schools followed.

Every school year was busy. The Calendar for 1922-3 is an example of the variety in work and play during a typical year:

**SCHOOL CALENDAR**
*Summer Term 1922*

| | | | |
|---|---|---|---|
| | May | 4 | *Beginning of Term* |
| | | 5 | *Distribution of Certificates by Miss Fry for 1920-21* |
| | | 31 | *Geography Expedition to Clent* |
| | June | 5, 6, 7 | *Whitsuntide Holiday* |
| | | 16 | *Gymnastic Competition* |
| | | | *Old Girls' Play* |
| | | 17 | *Old Girls' Association Meeting* |
| | | 27 | *History Club 'Midsummer Revels'* |
| | | 30 | *Dancing and Gymnastic Display* |
| | July | 4 | *Higher School Certificate Examination* |
| | | 7 | *Choir Concert* |
| | | 11 | *Oxford Senior Local Examination* |
| | | | *Cricket Match – School v Fathers* |

|  |  |  |
|---|---|---|
|  | 20 | Prefects' Party |
|  | 21 | English Club Performance of 'As You Like It' |
|  | 24 | Election of Prefects 1922-23 |
|  | 25 | French Play |
|  | 26 | End of Term |

**Autumn Term 1922**

|  |  |  |
|---|---|---|
| September | 14 | Beginning of Term |
| November | 6 | Half Term Holiday |
|  | 10 | Distribution of Certificates by Miss Robertson |
| December | 13, 14, 15, 16 | Performance of 'Julius Caesar' |
|  | 20 | End of Term |

**Spring Term 1923**

|  |  |  |
|---|---|---|
| January | 11 | Beginning of Term |
|  | 13 | Old Girls' Association Party |
|  | 27 | Dr Blaker's Lecture on 'The Care of the Teeth' |
|  | 28 | Lecture on 'The Battle of Jutland' |
| February | 1 | Mr and Miss Howe's Lecture and Concert |
|  | 12 | Examinations |
|  | 19 | Half Term Holiday |
|  | 23 | Upper Fifth Dance |

| | | |
|---|---|---|
| March | 2 | Upper Fourth Dance |
| | 16 | Parents' Day – Exhibition of Work |
| | 17 | Expedition to see Drinkwater's 'Oliver Cromwell' |
| | 21 | Dancing Display |
| | 22 | English Club Performance of 'The Piper' |
| | 28 | End of Term. |

The early 1920's saw the development of the Pioneer Club – a DGHS version of the Guides, which had begun in 1918 with 20 Brownies and 25 Guides.

"*The girls were amalgamated into patrols to learn such useful accomplishments as bandaging, cooking, washing and ironing. Weekly meetings seemed to be a preparation for womanhood. 'We learnt how to lay a table properly, to cook several dishes and to spring clean a room. Mrs Seager instructed us in the mysteries of bathing and dressing a baby.' But it was not all work for the Pioneers. They had many enjoyable tracking expeditions over Wrens Nest and very exciting times on the Castle, where they played 'storming the Castle'.*"

Highlights of the Pioneers' year were the camps held in the summer holidays. The first camp was held at Lowestoft in 1920 and others followed at Holly Bush, Sutton Park, Enville, Hope Bowdler and Stroud. In 1924 Patrol Leaders and seconds spent a weekend at Miss Frood's cottage, 'The Beehive', near Halfpenny Green.

At the beginning of the Summer term of 1923, the Prince of Wales visited Dudley. The School turned out in full force to welcome him. All along Priory Road and Ednam Road the girls sat patiently on their satchels, waiting for their hero to pass by. As his car approached, the girls cheered wildly. But what they had all looked forward to for so long was over, it seemed, in a moment. And, perhaps a little dejectedly, they all returned to School.

Miss Norton and some of the Upper School helped with the 'International Survey of the Sky' from the 24th to the 28th September 1923. As voluntary surveyors, they took cloud photographs at regular intervals throughout the day. These pictures formed part of the British contribution to the World collection.

**Pioneer Club – Sutton 1923**

**Waiting for the Prince of Wales 1923**

A Verse-Speaking Competition held at the Temperance Hall in Walsall in the same year was judged by the poet, John Masefield. Seven aspirants went to the preliminary adjudication and two in the 15-18 Class survived for the final round – one received a certificate and the other high praise from the poet.

In December 1923, the School gave four performances of Shakespeare's *A Midsummer Night's Dream*. The proceeds, amounting to £51.12.0, were divided between the Mayor's Relief Fund and a contribution towards the purchase of the Encyclopaedia Britannica for the School – the first time that it made itself a gift.

**'A Midsummer Night's Dream' 1923**

**Sixth Form picnic 1924**

As early as 1917, Marion Richardson's work as teacher of Art at the School became familiar to the London artist, Roger Fry. In 1919, he invited her to exhibit some of the Dudley children's paintings in London at the Omega Workshop. In 1923, an Exhibition consisting entirely of paintings by Dudley High School girls, held at the Independent Gallery in London, attracted considerable attention. Following this exhibition, Miss Richardson's fame as a teacher of Art to children spread far and wide.

Marion Richardson came to the School in 1912. She was the youngest member of Miss Frood's staff, and was full of enthusiasm for her subject. The secret of her success was her respect for her pupils' work. She took great care in selecting subjects and scenes for girls to use in their lessons. The Bible and the poems of Keats, Shelley, Wordsworth and Coleridge were all sources of inspiration.

**Marion Richardson**

"*Marion often went to London after school to see the Russian Ballet, returning late and walking from Dudley Port. Next day she gave the girls vivid word-pictures of the ballets she had seen, which were translated into paintings.*"

The studio was a place of peace and security, as Marion Richardson taught with sympathy, understanding and encouragement. Gaily-painted cupboards and pictures added to the beauty of the Studio. Elsewhere in School the art work could be seen in hand-printed curtains in the Staff room, Library and Headmistress's room. The studio also played an important part in the production of plays. Scenery, furniture and dresses with bold designs on stiff muslin, giving the appearance of rich brocade, were all produced in the studio.

In 1930 she became a Lecturer at the London Day Training College and, three years later, Art Inspector for the London County Council. She retired early owing to ill health and returned to Dudley to be cared for by her friend, Miss Plant. Shortly before her death she said:

**"***And once again I am under the magic spell of Dudley.***"**

In September 1924 three of the Staff were laid low with Scarlet Fever, in those days a highly contagious disease. The School was closed for a week, but Staff continued to be affected for much longer and, sadly, Miss D Taylor died as a result of the illness.

A group of Board of Education Inspectors descended on the School in the Spring Term of 1925 for a General Inspection. The School, as usual, rose to the occasion and was congratulated in the report

**The Studio**

**Cupboard painting**

on general tone and for highly satisfactory work, with 'outstanding excellence' in History, Art, Writing and Domestic Science.

A new venture in 1926 was the School Album, which meant that records of school activities could be kept by means of photographs as well as accounts in *The Cornflower*.

In March 1926, The Shakespeare Memorial Theatre in Stratford-upon-Avon burnt down. The English Club decided to do something to help the New Theatre Fund in the summer of that year. With the help of the Folk-Dancing Club, they devised a Shakespeare afternoon. The programme included the presentation of a scene from *A Winter's Tale*, which involved several country dances. The Folk-Dancing Club bought material and made Elizabethan costumes to add to the impact of the play. As a result of the display – and tea and competitions – a substantial donation was sent to the New Theatre Fund.

The New Shakespeare Memorial Theatre was opened on the anniversary of Shakespeare's birthday in 1932. The streets of Stratford were lavishly decorated with evergreens, spring flowers and wreaths sent by those who had helped to finance the building. The quotation attached to the laurel wreath from the School was *'His leaf shall not wither'*. Members of the School were there to witness the celebrations and the opening by the Prince of Wales.

**Science Laboratory 1927**

The General Strike in 1926 brought its own problems for the School. Despite a lack of public transport, girls were determined to reach School somehow, sometime, although for those who always walked to School, each day was just an 'ordinary' day. There was little interruption to school routine except that the day ended at 3.00pm. As the strike continued, girls were helped on their way to School, sometimes rattling in an old Ford van or enjoying the luxury of a car. At 3.00pm, everyone met in the Hall in area groups – Tipton, Coseley, Brierley Hill – and gradually the girls were taken home. Only the town girls were left to walk. The all-important question, 'Is the miner or the mine-owner right?' was often discussed. A collection in the form of a line of pennies was made for the children of the local miners. When the strike was eventually over everyone felt very relieved, but life seemed suddenly very uninteresting.

**Arbor Day 1926**

A happier event of 1926 was Arbor Day held on 22nd November, when trees were planted to form a screen between the allotments and the hockey field. The gardening captains had the honour of planting the trees, which had been given by staff and girls. Miss Burke, the former Headmistress had given a rowan tree, *'a tree which thrives well in the climate and soil of Dudley'*. Almost 50 years later a similar event took place when the Governors, Parents, Miss Fisher, the Staff, Miss Sarmiento and Girls presented trees for the School grounds.

A Scholarship and Loan Fund was set up in 1927 to give financial assistance to girls to enable them to stay on longer at school, go to college, or train for their future careers. There were few other grants available at that time.

A former pupil who achieved outstanding success in the 1920's was Mary Percy. In 1927, Mary qualified as a doctor at the University of Birmingham, winning the Queen's Prize for the highest combined marks in Medicine, Surgery and Obstetrics. She decided to spend a year in Alberta, Canada, after seeing an advertisement in the *British Medical Journal,* and was sent to the Battle River district of Northern Alberta. In 1931, she married Frank Jackson, a fur trader and farmer from Keg River, where she practised medicine for the next 43 years, dedicating herself to the fight against TB and rabies, as well as treating the settlers and the native people of the region.

**Mary Percy**

Her achievements were recognised with many awards. In 1967, she was presented with the Centennial Medal of Canada *'in recognition of her valuable service to the nation'.* In 1975, together with her husband, she was given the Alberta Achievement Award and named 'Woman of the Year' for the *Voice of Native Women.* In 1976, she was named an Officer in the Order of Canada, and the insignia was presented to her by the Governor General.

**Line of pennies for Scholarship and Loan Fund**

Mary died in May 2000 at the age of 95. The Bishop of Peace River conducted the funeral service at the town of Manning, where her shack was the only building when she was posted there. There was only one other doctor between there and the North Pole. Mary's life story *The Home Made Brass Plate*, was written by Cornelia Lehn and published in 1988.

Staff are remembered long after they leave the School, some names, together with associated stories, remaining well-known years later by people who had never known them individually. DGHS has been fortunate in the number of Staff who have served the School for long periods, often 20 years or more. The following pen portraits recall some of the 'names' of the 1920-40 era.

Margaret Silvers wrote in *The Cornflower* of Miss Fiske (1922-45):

"*She was full of the most unexpected surprises – tea (with cherries) on the lawn during Higher School Certificate week for her Sixth Form, or at her house (with ice cream) for her Third Form. In fact she was the perfect school mistress, which means that she was entirely unlike one...*

*I mostly wondered at her tolerance, not only of us (and we must have needed much tolerating) but of ideas. We so often got dogmatic and indignant in arguments which seemed to range from religion to politics (for we managed to cover a good many more subjects than literature in her lessons), but she had that rare power of understanding and sympathising with both sides.*

*Her lessons were a delight. From the very earliest days when we read 'Sir Patrick Spens' in a very false Scots accent and stumbled through 'A Midsummer Night's Dream' we enjoyed them because she was enjoying them. In all her dealings, though she could most certainly see the worst side of us, she had the capacity of always believing in the best.*"

Miss Goddard (1919-44) joined the staff as School Secretary and later became Second Mistress. Younger children, who had known her from the time when – rather frightened – they entered the School, were much attracted by her kind smile and fascinating ear-rings. Higher up the School it was her humour and the variety in her lessons that were appreciated. Suspense is attractive and pupils never knew what might come next in a lesson. Miss Frood recalled that there were harrowing moments:

❝*Miss Goddard had a way of letting one know of some trivial mishap with the exaggerated phrase, 'Something perfectly appalling has happened. I am most terribly sorry,' and then, as one steeled oneself to the idea of a child having broken an arm or leg in the playground, she would add in the same tone of horror, 'I have a blot in my register.*❞

Miss Goddard's help with play productions and games coaching was also much appreciated.

Arriving at the same time as Miss Goddard was Miss Plant (1919-44), affectionately known as 'Polly Plant', who 'mothered' many boys and girls in their early years in school. She was hardly ever irritated and regarded any small boy or girl, however tiresome, as an individual whose reactions were bound to be interesting and instructive. She never worried about the clock, so always paid grave attention to every remark addressed to her, and remained calm even in the inevitable crises.

A pupil recalls how she enjoyed Miss Plant's lessons, from standing on a chair and writing in the air to reciting what she had for breakfast without saying 'um'. Miss Plant was an outstanding teacher of Art and handwriting and worked with Miss Marion Richardson in producing the *Dudley Handwriting* books. Miss Frood contributes to the portrait with this comment taken from *The Cornflower* of 1944:

> *Many an Old Girl will associate with Miss Plant the question 'And what are you doing here, my dear?' addressed indiscriminately to the august Prefect on duty or the young person illegally taking a short respite from the boredom of the classroom.*

When Miss Vincent (1920-45) left, Miss Chilton wrote in *The Cornflower:*

> *Miss Vincent was so much part of the life of DGHS that it was very difficult for all who had worked with her to accustom themselves to her absence. The Junior School, particularly, felt lost without her vigour and purpose to guide them, and she was sadly missed in the Senior School whenever stage scenery had to be reared or parties arranged. No girl or boy who passed through her classes could forget her phenomenal patience over difficulties in Arithmetic, nor the fun and stimulus of her approach to History.*

In a later issue of *The Cornflower*, Miss Bate, the School Secretary, adds to the picture:

> *Behind a somewhat stern manner Miss Vincent had a warm heart, and was very much concerned with the welfare of her Lower Third and of the School as a whole.*

The first Assistant Mistress to complete 21 years of service at DGHS was Miss Worster (1917-38). She taught in the Junior School and later became its Head, deputising for Miss Frood when necessary at parent interviews. She helped to form the Home and School Council and was a keen supporter of the Old Girls' Association.

Writing in *The Cornflower*, Miss Chilton recalled Miss Worster's method of highlighting to the HMI the problems of accommodation:

> *The distance to the lavatories and the rest room constituted another problem. Miss Worster, determined to*

demonstrate the situation, arranged for the usual mass pilgrimage of seven-year-olds in the Annexe to take place in the middle of a gym class. While the girls using apparatus were arrested in mid-action, the pilgrims crawled silently under the boom, returning several minutes later by the same route."

A winning entry in a poetry competition in 1929 throws some light on the staff:

**'THE PRESENT STAFF'**

A is Miss Atkinson, dark and tall,
B is Miss Buckingham, also Miss Ball,
C is Miss Clark, at whose subject we quake,
D with this letter there's no name to take.
E there is none, so take F in its stead,
F is Miss Fiske and Miss Frood, who's their head.
G is Miss Goddard, many lessons she takes,
H is Miss Haslehurst, mathematicians she makes,
I, J, and K, none. Pass on to Miss Lodge,
L for her Latin which we'd love to dodge,
M is Miss Mathews, who's been here a year,
N is Miss Norton, whom we all love and fear.
O's Miss O'Dwyer, who in gym won't take 'can't',
P is Miss Pattison, Miss Pierce and Miss Plant,
Q we're afraid we have no one to quote on,
R for Miss Richardson, also Miss Roughton,
S is Miss Stirk, who took us to Paris (ee),
T we have no one, so here we won't tarry,
U of that name the Staff are quite innocent,
V's Miss De Vesian and also Miss Vincent,
W is Miss Worster, Miss Whitfield, Miss Ward,
X, Y and Z, there are none on the board.

Dear Staff, if you read this, do not be annoyed,
For it was a temptation we could not avoid.

(S G M and D V G – Lower Five P)

**Alderman Smellie**

Norwood, 17 St James's Road, was a house acquired by the School in about 1915 to provide accommodation for members of staff, since in those days there were no opportunities for single women to buy or rent houses; the only possibility was to live with a land-lady. There were a number of bed-sitting rooms and a common dining room. In the early days there were maids living on the top floor. Later on a daily cleaner serviced the rooms. Usually the German and French assistants lived there too. The staff lived as a family group and took turns to set the menus – doing the shopping and cooking and, of course, the washing-up in the latter days.

Alderman James Smellie was Chairman of the Governing Body from 1924 to 1944. The James Smellie Medal was an annual award for the girl who had given the best service to the School during the year and was presented to her at Speech Day. The earliest record of its presentation is in 1929.

Alderman F W Cook was a governor of the School for 15 years. His store in Dudley High Street was, for many years, the official stockist of the DGHS uniform. The store organised an advertisement competition but, unfortunately, there is no record of the result.

On 19th February 1930 The Distribution of Certificates took place at the New Town Hall. Dr Barnes, Bishop of Birmingham, presented the certificates, cups and sums of money gained by various girls in payment for dress material, painted trays and bowls. He was presented with a leather portfolio made by the Junior School, and Mrs Barnes with, of all things, a kettle holder!

## SPORT

Throughout the lifetime of the School physical education played an important part. Prior to 1900, it is recorded in Blocksidge's Almanac:

*"Great attention is paid to the physical training of the pupils – a special class for gymnastics is held during the winter months, while drilling lessons form a regular part of the school work, and the large play-ground and tennis court give ample opportunity for out-door exercise."*

The first issue of *The Cornflower* in December 1913 records Netball results and that Hockey had begun in real earnest. By 1918 Tennis, Cricket, Netball and Hockey had become a part of School life and the first Rounders matches were recorded in 1925. This game became more important after cricket had been abandoned owing to the difficulty of arranging fixtures with other schools. Inter-form competitions in all sports took place and Inter-school results were given in the School magazine, as were criticisms of individual team members.

In 1926, DGHS pupil Dorothy Round was said to *"...have improved tremendously since last year and promises to become*

**F.W. COOKS**

**Offer Three Prizes**

**1st 10/-    2nd 7/6    3rd 5/-**

for the most original advertisements of their Business, describing the advantages of shopping at Cook's, and what can be bought there.

*The following are the Conditions :—*

1. —The effort, which can be illustrated, must be composed by a girl attending the Dudley Girls' High School, and be done without assistance.

2. —The advertisement must be suitable for insertion in a full page of "The Cornflower" and, if approved, will become the property of F. W. Cook Ltd., for reproduction in the Press.

3. —The Advertising Manager of the "Dudley Herald" has kindly consented to act as Judge and his decision must be accepted as final.

*All Efforts should be posted before August 30th*

*to—*

**F. W. COOK LTD.**
GIRLS' SCHOOL OUTFITTERS,
——DUDLEY——

*a distinguished player."* Eight years later, on the fence in front of the School, there appeared in large letters, '6-2, 5-7, 6-3. *Bravo Dorothy'.* She had won the Wimbledon Ladies' Final!

Dorothy Round's association with DGHS began in 1915. She was good at all sports and played in the hockey teams with pace and dash. It was at tennis however that she showed extraordinary ability. With much practice and hard work she improved tremendously during her school years. In 1926 she reached the semi-final in the Junior Championships at Wimbledon and a year later took part in the Wightman Cup.

**Dorothy Round Finalist 1933**

**Dorothy Round winning Wimbledon 1934**

In 1931-32 she reached the last eight in the Wimbledon Championships. Dorothy maintained her links with School and returned to take part in an exhibition tennis match during the Jubilee Celebrations. Success continued and in 1934 Dorothy won the Ladies' Single Title and the Mixed Doubles. In 1937 she again won the Ladies' Singles Championship. Her five Wimbledon titles – two singles and three doubles – were more than any other English woman had achieved since the First World War, a record still standing into the start of the third Millennium.

The School commemorated Dorothy's victories by placing a bronze tablet in the entrance hall and by the introduction of the Dorothy Round Singles Championship. The trophy, in the form of a shield, was presented annually. Dorothy maintained her links with the School and was an active member of the Old Girls' Association.

The prized Dorothy Round shield was first played for in 1935, and the final became a major occasion every summer, watched by the whole School. Heather Cartwright, who won the shield in 1964, was selected to play in the Girls' Doubles at the Junior Wimbledon Championships.

Another successful sportswoman was Hildred Freakley, who played for England against Ireland in an international Lacrosse match at Dublin in 1938.

**The Dorothy Round Shield won by Heather Cartwright**

**Dorothy Round presenting the Shield to Rosemary Harrison**

Hockey was particularly popular in the 1950's and several girls reached County level, with the enthusiastic coaching of Miss June Howard, herself a first-class goal-keeper. 1953 saw the start of what was to become an annual pilgrimage to see a Women's Hockey International at Wembley. Never before can the ground have experienced the sound of such ear-piercing, high-pitched cheering!

The School began taking an active interest in Athletics in 1957 and, after a new jumping pit and running track had been provided, training began in earnest. The School won the cup at the Dudley School Sports for many years in succession, and similar success was achieved in the Dudley Schools' Swimming Sports. In the 1960's, Friday Club afforded opportunities for taking part in more unusual sports such as Fencing, Judo and Archery. Some of the Sixth Form also tried their hand at Golf

**Dan Maskell shows new coaching methods**

**Country dancing 1927**

Corner of Hall/Gymnasium 1927

The Strokemaster 1962

Rounders team 1961

Hockey team 1916

Hockey team 1959-1960

and there are memories of one beginner coming back from the course triumphant in that she had achieved a 'hole in 17'!

One of the School's problems was the playing field:

**"***The field proved so full of daisies and plantain that the cricket team could not show its real form. Something had to be done and the whole school did it. One afternoon armed with a daisy grubber or an old table fork every girl sallied forth, found the square of turf, miraculously marked out for her form, and dug with good will that sprang partly from enthusiasm for the task, but partly from the pleasure of broken routine.***"**

**Cricket team 1939**

**Tennis team 1931**

## 'WEED FEVER BY NON WASTE-FIELD'

*I must go down to the field again, to the field where the plantains lie,*
*And all I ask is a basket, soil, and a knife to dig or die,*
*And a warm coat for the wind's song doth send me cold and shaking,*
*And a green mist before my eyes, and the weeds the ground forsaking.*

*I must go down to the field again, for the call of the Weed Campaign,*
*Is a wild call and a clear call that sounds again and again,*
*And all I ask is a sunny day with a light breeze sighing,*
*And the green grass and the brown earth, and the plantains dying.*

*I must go down to the field again,*
*to the muddy life I love,*
*('Tis the worm's way on a warm day*
*when a shower falls from above),*
*And all I ask is a merry yarn from*
*a laughing fellow weeder,*
*And a soft sigh and a brave cry,*
*'Come! Follow the campaign leader.'*

(Christine Poulson,
Upper Fourth 3 – July 1934)

**The Plantains 1934**

**DANCE**

Whilst on a visit to her sister in Russia, Miss Frood was introduced to the modern dance work pioneered by Laban and Jooss – Jewish teachers who had been teaching in Germany and had escaped to political exile in London. Joan Goodrich had worked with Laban and Jooss in Germany and she went on to teach dance at Bedford College. One of Joan Goodrich's students there in 1933-36 was Edwina Angus, who came to teach PE and modern dance at DGHS. She stayed at Dudley until 1944. Phil Read also attended Bedford College and then taught at DGHS from 1945-48. She came to Dudley with a similar enthusiasm for modern dance. Ann Burleigh succeeded Phil Read and continued what was, by then, a tradition in the School and in other schools in the Borough which adopted modern dance.

In the 1940's, the School was one of a number considered to represent the country in Gymnastics and modern dance at the Linguad in Stockholm. However, Miss Burleigh and Veida Barclay were

**Gymnastics – Middle School 1938**

**European Dancing – Upper School 1939**

chosen as members of the Keep Fit team. For many years Miss Ellis served as accompanist, as well as giving piano lessons, and was an invaluable addition and support to the teaching of modern dance.

> *I remember having our dance lessons near the boys' school and hearing one of the boys describe us as 'pregnant fairies'. The piano stayed outside all summer – no one touched it, and Miss Ellis thumped away wearing thick cardigans, while we wore our blue tunics.*

### ANNIVERSARIES AND CELEBRATIONS

The 1930's provided several occasions for rejoicing. On 6th June 1931 the School celebrated its Golden Jubilee. The day began with a service in the Parish Church conducted by Canon Philips and attended by many former Staff, Old Girls and parents as well as the present Staff and pupils. In the afternoon a Garden Party was held in the School grounds, when Alderman Cook presented Miss Frood with the

**Dorothy Round Exhibition Tennis Match**

**The Staff – July 1931**

mallet used to lay the Foundation Stone of the School in 1910. The day ended with a Jubilee supper served in the Hall. Several after-dinner speeches were given by Old Girls and former Staff who recalled their happy days at DGHS.

Marion Richardson said that she always measured other places in terms of Dudley. It seemed to her that it would have been impossible for her to do her present job without having been there. The celebrations concluded with a concert given by Miss Vincent, Miss Cronin and several Old Girls. It had been a great day – one on which many old acquaintances were renewed, and one on which many claimed themselves proud to have been associated with the School.

The Silver Jubilee of George V was celebrated in 1935. By fortunate coincidence the School had recently acquired a radiogram and was able to listen to Commander King-Hall describing the scene in Westminster Hall, as loyal addresses were presented to the King. Every girl was presented with a copy of *The King's Grace* by John Buchan – a gift from the Education Committee.

To celebrate the Coronation of George VI in 1937, over 200 girls visited London and Windsor on 19th May. The party travelled by train to Marlow, where they boarded a steamboat for Windsor. "The inhabitants of the little town, seeing so many girls at a time, came out of their ivy and jasmine-covered houses to discuss us with their neighbours as we went by."

Miss Frood celebrated 25 years as Head with an Old Girls' party on 13th May 1939. Some former members of Staff had travelled long distances to be there and over 200 guests attended. Many tributes were paid to Miss Frood including one from Miss Taylor:

*"No one, she said, could fail to realise the intense vitality and vivid personality which Miss Frood possesses.*

*Her enthusiasm, which swept all obstacles before her, and her whole-hearted interest in everything relating to her work had enabled her, during this time, to carry the School along from strength to strength.* "

The ever-increasing demand for places at DGHS resulted in a need for building expansion. In 1936 two new form rooms, a dining room and kitchen were built as an extension on the North Wing. Mr and Mrs Bradney moved into a new house in the School grounds. The former Dining Hall became the Domestic Science room. The Sixth Form, who had used the Library as its base, moved into 1SE and the Library became a real library. But the long awaited and much needed gymnasium was not part of the building programme, much to Miss O'Dwyer's disappointment.

**The new Dining Hall 1939**

**The new wing – 1937**

## DRAMA

The period between the two World Wars witnessed a growth in the significance of drama in the School. A Literary and Dramatic Club was formed in 1917, with active participation of both Staff and girls. *The Taming of the Shrew* was read to the School and in 1918 the Staff performed *Alice in Wonderland*, raising £35 for St Dunstan's.

The English Club continued giving performances throughout the 1920's and 30's. These included a production of *The Alcestis of Euripides*, *Arms and the Man* and *Antigone*, and the Dramatic Club presented *The Barretts of Wimpole Street*. In 1936 the Staff read *Lady Precious Stream*, and the Dramatic Society gave a performance of *The Duenna*, which was later performed to the public, this being a first

**'Alcestis of Euripides' 1928**

**'Tobias and the Angel' 1937**

'Twelfth Night' 1926

'Lady Precious Stream' 1936

Sixth Form picnic with Miss Frood

for the Society. In 1937, the School play was *Tobias and the Angel.* From refugees to Jane Austen may seem a far cry, but it was due to the need to raise funds in aid of Jewish refugees that, in 1939, the Dramatic Club gave a public performance of an adaptation of *Pride and Prejudice.*

As rumours of war became an increasing concern it was suggested that an air-raid shelter should be built, giving rise to an ominous remark in *The Cornflower:*

**"***When this has been built... I suppose... the School will have air-raid drill instead of fire drill.***"**

**The Staff in 1941**

## Section Four

# Wartime 1939-1945

ONE OF THE MOST IMPORTANT EVENTS within the School during the Second World War was the retirement of Miss Frood and the appointment of her successor Miss Ambrose (1941-1964). At a Service of Thanksgiving for the life of Mary Ambrose, held in St Thomas's Church, Dudley, on 5th May 2000, Miss Beryl Fisher gave the address:

*I am very aware of the privilege I have been given today, but also very conscious of the responsibility and the difficult (I feel like saying the impossible) task of doing justice to the contribution Miss Ambrose made to Dudley Girls' High School, education in general and life in Dudley.*

*It is 50 years since I first met Miss Ambrose, having been invited to an interview for a teaching post. I remember it well. Miss Ambrose sitting at her table, talking and asking a few questions, which seemed fairly harmless at the time. Looking back I realised that she had found out a lot about me, what I knew and even more what I didn't! – so I was surprised to be offered the job. Typical of Miss Ambrose that it was a long time before she let out that I was the only applicant!*

*Born in Scotland, Miss Ambrose enjoyed school and Edinburgh University, where academic study gave her much satisfaction and a first-class honours degree in English Literature and Language. So began her passion for the subject. I think it was a desire to share this with others and her interest in people that led her into teaching.*

*Reading continued to be a pastime of Miss Ambrose and she enjoyed a wide variety of books. Poetry was much enjoyed and, when eyesight made reading difficult for her, I suggested a tape cassette, but the idea was scorned. 'I'd rather recite them to myself,' she said, 'I can remember them.' Nurses were staggered at the amount she could recall when in her mid-90's.*

*Many of us have been chided at some time for careless pronunciation – 'February' being one of her pet words and only a few months ago she told me she was trying to get a nurse to say it properly. Once a teacher always a teacher!*

*She wrote her funeral instructions and a brief summary of her life, called 'a record of the non-events of my 92 years'. She may not have hit the tabloid headlines, nor even the 'Dudley Herald', but her life was eventful in the way in which her influence inspired, changed and helped so many people.*

**Miss Ambrose**

*DGHS was a forward-looking school when she came in 1941. Miss Frood had a vision way ahead of the general education of the day, but Miss Ambrose developed that further in her own way. She had a desire to educate the whole person, not just concentrate on academic achievement, although that was high on the list, a desire that each girl should reach her potential and become a well-balanced responsible person. School and form council (she thought council sounded less judicial than court) encouraged an individual to express herself, to have an opinion, take part in discussion and vote in a democratic way. Time spent discussing choice of material for summer uniform or hats v berets was all part of growing up. I'm sure that many former council secretaries have found themselves called upon to write minutes in later life.*

*There was her keen support for activities that other grammar schools might have considered less important in school life. Music, of which she was very fond and knowledgeable, was important. She frequently recalled with pleasure the choir performances, concerts, musical productions of Gilbert and Sullivan, when the Grammar School and fathers were invited to join in drama productions, especially Shakespeare, speech competitions and writing competitions.*

She was small in stature but absolutely in command of the School without appearing to dominate it. There might have been fear and trepidation when sent for, but a firm, fair and understanding reception awaited one. I can't remember ever seeing her lose her temper, but she could express her dislike or disapproval, sometimes in a throw-away remark. A walk down the corridor to give a message to a member of staff was a good way of seeing what was going on in classrooms. Very little missed her eye or ear. She knew everything that was happening because she was interested.

The interest and support felt by staff was also acknowledged by pupils who look back in amazement at the speed with which she got to know the new intake, followed them through their school life, encouraged them in their career choice, often persuading hesitant parents that their daughter really ought to go on to higher education, knowing their families and remembering it all. Her memory was incredible right to the end and I certainly used her as my memory bank for years.

Sue Lawley once wrote to her: 'I had so much respect for you but never more than when I fell out of a tree in the midst of exam and revision time. You dusted me down, gave me a stick of barley sugar and just told me to get on with my work.' Sympathy combined with sound practical sense!

'Religious Education lessons with Miss Ambrose were always good. We were encouraged to discuss. Discussions often strayed from original matter but in the process we were helped to make a satisfying code of life.' She herself had a strong faith which guided her outlook on life and the way in which she lived it so that much was caught not taught. As someone said, 'Her kindly manner and firmly-held principles were admired and appreciated.' 'Miss Ambrose and the School opened doors for me that I never knew existed,' wrote another old girl. 'Miss Ambrose and the School were a ray of sunshine after my last school,' said a member of the staff.

*She had 35 years of retirement, all but the last three active. She enjoyed very much hearing from old girls and staff, especially if they had kept up their Marion Richardson writing, which was so readable. Two final quotes: 'DGHS was such a happy school', and 'A most wonderful Head, wise, calm and understanding'.*"

In 1938, DGHS, like the rest of Britain, began preparing for war. Writing 20 years afterwards, Miss Chilton remembered well the early stages:

"*At the time of the Munich Crisis, gas masks had arrived, and at twelve hours' notice we were required to fit all Dudley children with them. In theory I had supposed resignation would be preferable to training the young to such a devilish necessity. In practice, of course, I was only too anxious to learn how to fit them correctly. Then we had gas mask drill. To our relief, only one child under ten was upset by the first attempt to breathe with the whole face encased in rubber. The rest accepted the experiment without fuss. The trenches were dug, the digging being delayed by the shortage of rubber waders, since the subsoil was heavy clay, waterlogged at the depth of a few feet. The parents were appealed to, and several pairs of boots arrived on loan. The trenches were completed at the cost of £1000. Thereafter we had air raid drill, and presently the threat of raids themselves; plenty of guns, often planes, but no incidents. Dinner had occasionally to be served in the trenches, while we waited for the 'All Clear'. Great fun for the children, no doubt.*

*Next we were told that, while the likelihood of a direct hit was relatively remote, the possibility of windows being shattered from the blast of someone else's direct hit was not to be underestimated. So the girls were trained to take shelter from flying glass under their desks. Mr Bradney again functioned with a flag signal. Miss Read, merry and imperturbable Kindergarten mistress at this time, called me into NE to demonstrate her method of carrying out these hopeful instructions. The ideal Froebian class was before me, each child individually absorbed in some self-chosen and educative occupation. 'Children' says Miss Read, her voice at* its usual low level – pause – then in the same tone but, withal, a somewhat firmer enunciation 'Bombs'. Whereupon each child instantly ceased its play, crawled under its small table, and, turning into a brisk tortoise, crawled with 'house' to walls, the idea being that the glass blown inwards shoots into the centre of the room, obligingly falling short of any children under the opposite wall. Well, well! It didn't ever happen either.

Nor was it necessary for the School to be used as a hospital, though full preparations were made for the contingency. All the windows, including the very smallest, were blacked out by double dark green curtains with brass eyelets at intervals down each and every edge, and which hooked securely on to special battens down the sides of the window frames. The storage of these thousands of yards of material continued to be a problem for years after the war was over.

The Staff did firewatching on the premises at night, and the Handwork room became sleeping quarters for the four or five on duty. The steel girders were supposed to give a measure of safety. Part of the precautions included the reinforcing of the New Cloakroom ceiling because 'better' and faster aircraft were expected to reach us too rapidly to allow time for going to the trenches. So Mr Bradney was stationed at a strategic point with a flag, which he waved if he descried aircraft approaching. Someone watching his behaviour from N3 corridor had to blow a shrill fire whistle to alert the School. Then we all proceeded to the basement. Meanwhile Mr Bradney had taken all the Staff on personally conducted tours of the roof. If incendiary bombs fell during the night watches, Staff on duty were expected to hare up from the Handwork room, scale the ladder outside N1, cat-walk along the ceiling of the main corridor and, with Alpinists' balance and calm precision, hurl their sand bags (only portable by the balanced and robust), down an alarmingly steep and deep declivity on to the incendiaries, which would on occasion be lodged over the Hall. Well, this never happened – luckily for my reputation! "

Miss Bate, the School Secretary described how, for the first time, night became as important as day in the School:

"*Familiar objects seem strange when we prowl about in the darkness with just the little circle of light from our lamps to guide us. We are startled when we walk into something soft in the corridor, but it is only the black curtain by the hall. Imagined bursts of gunfire turn out to be but the reverberation of the windows from the passing of lorries some distance away. Firewatching has made us explore the mysteries of the roof, some of us needing courage to climb and descend the ladders. On moonlight nights the building and the grounds show a new beauty.*"

Miss Bate also wrote poignantly in the early stages of the War:

"*Perhaps we shall have our testing time in the future, when we shall need our tin hats and fire-fighting apparatus. Let us now prepare ourselves as far as we can and pray that we may act rightly if and when that time comes.*"

In fact fire-watching inspired a pupil, Joan Day, to write a poem which was published in *The Cornflower*:

**'IF' Dedicated to my fellow firewatchers**

> If you can man a stirrup-pump and shovel,
> > If you can dream, but not make dreams your aim,
> If in the pouring rain you earthward grovel,
> > Nor treat HE's and fire-bombs quite the same,
> If you can fight the flames and keep your virtue,
> > Talk with police, nor lose the common touch,
> If neither planes nor British flak can hurt you,
> > If wardens count with you – but not too much,
> If you can raise the bedsteads, varnished newly,
> > Walk on the roof, yet keep the floor in view,
> If you parade the grounds, returning duly,
> > With lumps of grass-court stuck upon your shoe,
> If you can climb the stairs in but a minute,
> > Your lamp attached, your hair within its curl,
> Yours is the School, and everything that's in it,
> > And, what is more, you'll get three shillings, girl!

The younger members of the School seem to have been more concerned with mundane matters, expressing regret that the bright hand-printed library curtains, designed by Marion Richardson, had given way to black-out, delight in an extra fortnight's holiday at the beginning of the Autumn term and the shortening of the school day, and disgust at the deterioration of school dinners.

Monica Homer wrote:

"School dinners were of great importance as we always seemed to be starving hungry. Although we criticized the meals most of us devoured everything served. All potatoes were cooked in their jackets and every bit was eaten. The cook's favourite salad was raw cabbage, which had no resemblance to today's coleslaw, it was just plain shredded cabbage. The desserts were planned to fill – suet pudding and jam sauce (one teaspoon of jam to a gallon of water) was a typical dish. Our sports mistress was annoyed when about an hour afterwards she had a class of rather lethargic girls, the after-effects of 'Spotted Dick' being very obvious."

Gradually the School adapted to a new way of life:

"We learned (slowly in some cases) to carry coats, and gas-mask cases containing, as well as gas masks, Pears soap and cotton wool. We wore identity discs. First Aid and Home Nursing courses were arranged and when the trenches were finished, in spite of the hardest winter in history, we had to practise going down them. Our out-of-school activities too had been changed: parties and clubs held in the evenings had to be cancelled, as the black-out of the hall was not completed until the end of the Spring term. Most of the staff were extensively engaged in ARP work, and gardening, which once occupied a modest place on the timetable, became a science for everyone."

Cooking too, became of even greater importance, and Miss Muffet gave lessons in war-time cookery. Needlework lessons were difficult owing to shortages, but Miss Mona Mathews, although a history teacher, found a market-trader who let her have lengths of material without coupons. They became known as 'Hitler's Bits'!

During the war years knitting became one of the most important activities, and some astonishing achievements are reported in *The Cornflower:*

"*Parcels of knitted garments have been sent at regular intervals to the Forces. The total number of garments knitted so far is three hundred and fifty. In response to Mrs Churchill's urgent appeal, forty pairs of oiled wool gloves were knitted in the last two weeks of the Autumn term and sent for the Russian soldiers.*"

Knitting competitions and knitting bees, however, can eventually lose their appeal and in 1945 we read that:

"*Two parcels, containing pullovers, socks, helmets, gloves and scarves, have been sent off in the course of the school year, but as yet we have not been able to meet the appeal for 150 cardigans for children in occupied Europe. However, we should like to thank our few stalwart supporters who have knitted so valiantly for this end.*"

Throughout the War great efforts were made to raise funds, not only for buying wool, but for many causes. A typical list of monies raised was published in 1940.

## COLLECTIONS.

The following collections were made during the year ending March 31st, 1940: —

|  | £ | s. | d. |
|---|---|---|---|
| Guest Hospital | 0 | 7 | 9 |
| Rhondda Valley Unemployed | 0 | 16 | 3 |
| Sunshine Home for Blind Babies | 0 | 11 | 6 |
| People's Dispensary for Sick Animals | 0 | 5 | 6 |
| St. Dunstan's | 0 | 2 | 6 |
| British Legion Poppy Day Fund | 1 | 15 | 0 |
| British Red Cross | 8 | 8 | 8 |
| Blue Cross | 0 | 2 | 0 |
| Polish Relief Fund | 3 | 10 | 0 |
| Turkish Relief Fund | 5 | 10 | 0 |
| Lord Baldwin's Refugee Fund | 5 | 8 | 3 |
| Finnish Relief Fund | 1 | 13 | 4 |
| SPECIAL EFFORTS | | | |
| For the Refugees: | | | |
|   Entertainment—Upper III.3. | 3 | 3 | 0 |
|   Ping-Pong Tournament | 0 | 18 | 0 |
|   Concert by Music Staff | 3 | 6 | 6 |
|   Photograph Competition | 0 | 11 | 0 |
|   Garden Fête—Lower IV.s. | 3 | 3 | 0 |
|   Cake Stands painted by Studio | 1 | 5 | 6 |
| For the Wool Fund: | | | |
|   Sale of Toffee—L.V.A. | 3 | 10 | 0 |
|   Mile of Pennies—U.IV.1. and U.IV.3. | 1 | 14 | 5 |
|   Sale of Newspapers | 4 | 10 | 4 |
|   Concert—L.III. | 2 | 5 | 2 |
|   Ping-Pong Tournament | 1 | 6 | 3 |
|   Pancake Party | 2 | 0 | 1 |
|   Fun Fair—U.Vth | 6 | 10 | 6 |
|   Magazine—U.IIIrds | 0 | 15 | 0 |
| | £63 | 9 | 6 |

The Poultry Club was inaugurated in September 1940 when 95 enthusiasts enrolled. After a long period of waiting a large but very dirty henhouse arrived. There was much scraping and scrubbing and then on 28th November, 12 beautiful Rhode Island Red pullets made their appearance, bringing with them two eggs. 1053 eggs were laid during that year. Despite the Club's initial success, feed for the hens became scarce. It took over 100 eggs to provide custard tarts for one school dinner, so instead the School kitchen took up their dried egg allowance and the Club was disbanded in 1944.

One of the most successful events was Red Cross Day in 1943, when the then huge sum of £294 was raised by means of pony rides, sideshows, a pets' corner, a baby competition and a dance display, which ended with more than half the School taking part in the Cumberland Reel. Nearly 2000 visitors had tea. During the morning the Upper Sixth prepared innumerable sandwiches and stacked piles of cakes. Many tons of biscuits had been made, with the help of cookery classes. Parents gave generously from their provision stores, so that there was a good supply of food, and very little had to be bought despite rationing restrictions.

As the War continued it was decided to open the School for activities during the Summer holiday, but only about 40 girls took advantage of them. However, there were some enterprising ventures. At the beginning of 1943, following contact with the Ship Adoption Society, the *Pierre Loti*, a French corvette manned by an English crew was allotted to the School. A Committee was formed with representatives elected from each form. In addition to letters being written to the crew, competitions involving the collection of books, magazines, knitting and ship halfpennies were held in School, followed by letters of thanks from Captain J Milner.

By 1947 the ship had returned to peacetime activities, with communication between pupils and crew continuing. Accompanied by his wife, Captain Milner visited the School and presented a model of his ship – now the *Empire Gulliver*.

In 1951 a new ship the *TES Techarius*, an oil tanker, with Captain P H Maton in command, replaced the *Empire Gulliver* and the association continued throughout the 1950's. On 17th May 1954 pupils and staff visited the ship while it was being repaired at Birkenhead – coach fare to Birkenhead and return 11/- (55p)! Association with the ship continued throughout the 1950's.

Some girls spent time at a Harvest camp near Dunchurch. It obviously took a while for the rural community and Black Country girls to adapt to each other's ways. A sixth former, Beryl Jones, wrote:

**Captain and Mrs Milner on their School visit**

**Model of the 'Empire Gulliver'**

> *Much to my embarrassment, the farmer one day asked me to drive a horse and cart down to the field and load it. I was forced to admit that my education up till that time had not included driving a horse. His amazement at this admission was very great, but I did redeem my character to some extent later on when I learnt to drive the tractor. I found this job both much less strenuous and one requiring fewer powers of persuasion and patience, for, unlike the horses, the tractor did not stop to nibble the hedge every two or three yards, completely oblivious of the person standing ignominiously by its side.*

The convent where they stayed was isolated from towns, newspapers and wireless, but the evenings were not dull. There were four pianos at their disposal, and the nuns were so impressed by their singing that they asked for a concert to be arranged. The girls received their first insight into convent life by attending services.

At last the War was drawing to a close and Miss Clifford recalled:

> *When we returned in September, came the end of firewatching for Staff and Old Girls. Though no one is likely to lament the curious chilly stuffiness of that underground room, the creaking beds, the lingering smell of handwork and the restless mice – for we had little worse than that to put up with – Staff and Old Girls do miss the contact that this task gave.*

The Staff gave a 'goodbye social' to the Old Girls in recognition of their generous help. The blackout regulations were lifted, enabling more after-school activities – and detentions were introduced!

One important event of that year was the changing of the name of School Court to School Council in an attempt to awaken a living interest in the system of self government – one of the characteristics of DGHS. The changes in Government met with success and enlivened the proceedings of the newly-named Council.

*8th June, 1946*

TO-DAY, AS WE CELEBRATE VICTORY, I send this personal message to you and all other boys and girls at school. For you have shared in the hardships and dangers of a total war and you have shared no less in the triumph of the Allied Nations.

I know you will always feel proud to belong to a country which was capable of such supreme effort; proud, too, of parents and elder brothers and sisters who by their courage, endurance and enterprise brought victory. May these qualities be yours as you grow up and join in the common effort to establish among the nations of the world unity and peace.

*George R.I.*

The highlight of the Autumn Term was a production of *The Tempest*. Rehearsals began early in the term and everyone involved was very enthusiastic. The difficulties of making costumes during clothes rationing were overcome by using curtain materials and any scraps that could be begged or borrowed (surely not stolen), and soon the whole School seemed to be involved in some way.

The opening performance for the School was on 6th December, but at 4.30pm, to coincide with the start of *'Act l, Scene l. On a ship at sea, during a storm'*, the fog came down 'solidly' and the play was abandoned. Fortunately, the weather cleared and the next day the School saw the performance. The general public saw the play on 15th and 16th December and a profit of £56 was sent to charities.

Early in the Summer Term of 1945 everyone was in a state of suspense, as the end of the war approached. Some girls debated whether it was worthwhile doing homework as victory was imminent. Finally, on 8th May, VE Day was announced and the School had two days'

The Staff 1946

holiday. Later came celebrations with a picnic and sports on the field, but this was interrupted by heavy showers and meant picnicking indoors. The sun shone briefly on the obstacle bicycle race, the wheelbarrow race, the blindfold chariot race and the tug-of-war between the Staff and Sixth Form (won after a valiant fight by the stalwart Sixth). Then the rain descended. The weather had the last word yet again!

## Section Five

# Post-War Era 1945-1960

IT IS USUALLY ASSUMED by historians that 'The Sixties' was the time of social change and liberation, and that 'The Fifties' was, in contrast, dull and uneventful. A study of DGHS during the period 1945-1960 hardly merits this description and provides vivid memories for many Old Girls and Staff.

Hardly had the School settled into a peacetime routine when, in 1947, the weather presented another crisis:

*"In looking back at the events of this year there is one that looms prodigiously over everything else – the Great Cold Spell! It is always slightly exhilarating to experience something, however bad, which can be proudly labelled the Greatest or the Worst or the Largest in living memory. Writing this editorial in May sunshine in the garden does nothing to alleviate the retrospective miseries suffered during January, February and March. Even the usually enthusiastic Junior and Lower School were heard to admit that they were "sick of the snow." The School however displayed a magnificent determination not to be thwarted in its educational zeal. Those who could not get regular transport hewed and hacked, dug and hitch-hiked. At least one exit was made through a window when doors were blocked, and special mention must be made of the Upper Fifth who arrived punctually and practically en masse to do their examinations in some of the most unpleasant weather. Throughout we were cheered and sustained by warmth and sustenance produced for us by Mr and Mrs Bradney, without whose unflagging effort we should have suffered the major fate of frozen pipes and unheated buildings. For only two days the School was forced to close for lack of fuel."*

Five years later came our stormiest winter ever and the worst floods in Eastern England. As during wartime, the School raised a sizeable sum to send to Flood Relief.

Other national events were reflected in school life. In February 1950, the Lower Sixth were given a chance to run a political election in School, following as closely as possible the regulations governing Parliamentary elections. Two candidates stood for election, Jill Speake, Conservative and Ann Richardson, Labour.

Activities were limited by the rule that each party was not allowed to spend more than two shillings on election expenses and a restriction was made on the amount of paper to be used. Ten days before the polling Miss Ambrose, as Returning Officer, received the candidates, accompanied by their agents and their deposit of 3d. Both candidates addressed the eve-of-the-poll meeting with Miss Ambrose in the chair. Jill Speake gave full information on the critical situation at present and quoted facts about Conservative activity in the past. Like her opponent later, she had much to say on housing problems. Ann Richardson concentrated on the need for social planning to allow everyone the fullest opportunity for life. Polling began at 8.30am in the Handwork Room where separate polling booths were constructed. By 2pm all girls intending to vote had done so, the only abstentions two with Liberal sympathies.

The result:   Conservatives   148
              Labour          101

In the country's general election ten days later a Labour Government was elected. It is interesting to note that later Jill Speake became a doctor, and Ann Richardson, a solicitor.

The next year, the Festival of Britain was celebrated, marking the centenary of the Great Exhibition. The town celebrated by presenting a Pageant of Dudley in the Castle courtyard. On every evening for a week, nine episodes of Dudley history were enacted, from Saxon to Victorian times, and the large audiences who braved the chilly June evenings were delighted to recognize well-known Dudley people, who unexpectedly appeared on the stage in historical costume. Miss Ann Burleigh had trained a very large troupe of dancers from the School who took part in the Masque, accompanied by a full orchestra. The Pageant was a great success and one Junior pupil wrote triumphantly: *"It is over now, but I was in it, although I was only a tree."*

The Festival was also celebrated by the History Department, who presented an exhibition based on the town's Coat of Arms. A series of colourful posters showing the history of the town decorated the walls of the School.

**'Steel Chorus' Dudley Pageant 1951**

**Waiting for the Queen's visit to Dudley in 1957**

In 1953 came the Coronation of Queen Elizabeth II. Again an exhibition of beautifully-scripted posters was presented by the Sixth Form, and the Coronation Service became the subject of special lessons under the guidance of Miss Humphreys. The Chairman of the Governors presented each girl with a silver spoon, Dudley's gift to mark the occasion, and, most important, the School celebrated with three days' holiday, to enable those lucky enough to own a television, or to have a friend with one, to watch all the events on the tiny black-and-white screen.

During the Fifties the School buildings changed and expanded. No improvements had been possible for a long time, but now the School went through a period of regeneration after the constrictions of the War years. The earliest signs of this were when the girls returned to School in September 1949 to find two virtually new laboratories, which had changed places during the summer holidays. The Hall, Dining Room and Annexe were repainted during the Autumn term, and in the following weeks all the classrooms were redecorated.

Following the excitement of the Coronation, 1954 seems to have been a quieter year, but quieter may be the wrong word, for this was the year that the long-awaited new classrooms were built – North 5 and 6. The building began in January, but for some reason soon ceased and the work only started in earnest in the Summer Term and carried on through until Whitsuntide 1955, when the rooms were finally ready for use. The rooms sounded rather remote and cold and, in winter, they often did resemble polar regions. Two extra classrooms had been made available, but in reality only one, ISE, which had been the Sixth Form room, became a much needed Staffroom. The Sixth Form, much to their disappointment, were moved to ISI, a smaller room which had to accommodate the largest Upper Sixth on record.

There were also academic developments. The Spring Term of 1953 brought a full-scale visit of HM Inspectors to the School. The experience did not prove as daunting as everyone had feared, though daunting enough, and everyone was relieved when a good report followed.

❝*We felt we must have surpassed ourselves in deception, when we heard that our tidiness had been praised! The visitors said that they had enjoyed their week and found Dudley Girls' High School a happy place to work in.*❞

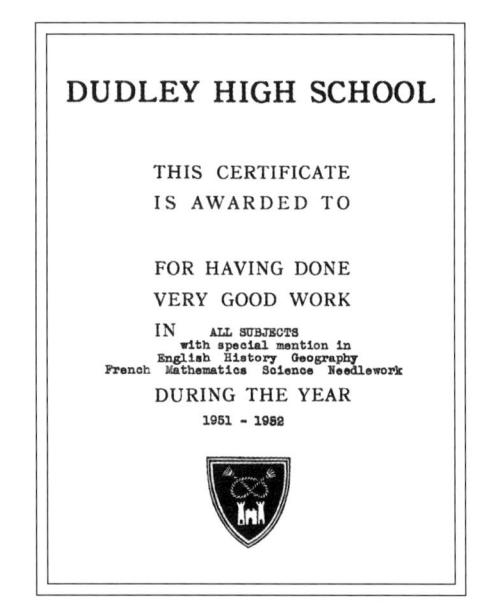

**DUDLEY HIGH SCHOOL**

THIS CERTIFICATE
IS AWARDED TO

FOR HAVING DONE
VERY GOOD WORK
IN     ALL SUBJECTS
   with special mention in
   English History Geography
French Mathematics Science Needlework
DURING THE YEAR
1951 – 1952

**Certificate for Good Work**

The decade had begun auspiciously with the first award of a State Scholarship. The achievement was repeated many times during the following ten years. New subjects were introduced into the curriculum – 'A' level Scripture, Spanish, Greek for some Lower Fifths, and a General course for Sixth Formers not taking external examinations. As in other schools the Fifth and Sixth Formers faced the new GCE examinations and were greatly concerned about being guinea pigs.

There were other changes which seemed important at the time. The timetable was adjusted on Wednesdays to allow for a preparation period at the end of the day so that team practices should not take girls away from vital lessons. Another change was a new scale of marks: grades A to C were replaced by five grades, A to E. This took some time to adjust to and parents at first were alarmed that the standard of their children's work had suddenly deteriorated overnight. Again, since the Preparatory Department had not been part of the School since 1944, it seemed more logical for new girls to enter the First Form instead of Upper Third and to rename the other forms accordingly. This was unpopular at first, especially with the Lower Fourth who became Third Formers when they went up! But, as with most changes, girls and staff soon adjusted.

There was one change, however, which brought about a rebellion. It remained the School's custom at Speech Days to award certificates for good work in individual subjects, and book prizes only to those who gained the best marks in public examinations. They took quite a long time to distribute, as about a third of the School received acknowledgement for their efforts and trooped across the platform of the Town Hall. Evenings were enlivened, especially for the younger girls, by the annual appearance of the Staff in their gowns and brightly-coloured or fur-trimmed hoods, and by a joyous rendering of *Jerusalem*.

**School report**

For some time it was thought that it would also be appropriate to sing a School Song or Hymn and in 1955 Miss O'Dwyer wrote the words of one, which was set to music by the Musical Advisor, Mr Vincent Knight.

Then came the dreadful news. Miss Ambrose had decided that the new hymn was to *replace* the singing of *Jerusalem* as she felt that 'dark, satanic mills' no longer had any relevance to the School. Immediately there were cries of indignation and general uproar. Eventually, as so often at DGHS, a compromise was reached and *both* were sung on Speech Day. It was reported that the new hymn had "a somewhat shabby rendering, but at the end of the evening the School rose to sing 'Jerusalem' with almost defiant vigour."

**SCHOOL HYMN**

*Lord, teach us love, that we may seek and find*
  *The lamp that Thou hast lit in all mankind;*
*That, learning, we may spend unselfishly*
  *Our lives for others, as we grow to Thee.*

*Lord, teach us courage, that we never lie*
  *To self or foe or friend, but carry high*
*Thy blade of truth, that nothing shall dismay*
  *Our hearts within Thy hand, who art the Way.*

*Lord, teach humility of mind and soul,*
  *That we may serve with heart and spirit whole,*
*Unflawed by arrogance or loud conceit,*
  *And lay Thy loan of knowledge at Thy feet.*

*Bless Thou, O Lord, this school in which our youth*
  *Is spent in glad endeavour; let Thy truth*
*Direct its life, as each succeeding age*
  *Shares this, our honour and our heritage.*

Times change and it is interesting to note that, 20 years later, when the School Hymn was dropped in favour of the Grammar School's *Ye Holy Angels Bright*, there was just as much dismay – this time with no reprieve. Today many Old Girls from that era recite Miss O'Dwyer's verses with looks of tearful nostalgia!

In 1946 Miss O'Dwyer organised a writing competition for the Easter holidays, to be judged by Marion Richardson, and below is an extract of the report she gave when judging the competition:

"*By taking a little trouble anyone can learn to write well, and you Dudley High School girls are wise in having done so and fortunate in being well-taught. Good writing is like good manners, something that we can all possess. However faithfully handwriting may follow a fine model, from the very first it will express the individuality of the writer and become more and more characteristic as experience and personality fill out. Never fear that by learning 'school' writing, which does acknowledge tradition, your writing will become dull and uniform. It is and will remain your very own.*

*There are many things that we shall never achieve. But to write a fair and seemly hand is well within our reach. Let us not neglect it. Let us employ it to express our delight in the dignity and orderliness of everyday things.*"

Despite the policy of not awarding form prizes, competition was encouraged and there was much rivalry between the 1's, 2's, and 3's. Once a year, in a Form Council period, silence reigned as every girl completed a page of her best handwriting for the Writing Competition. Miss O'Dwyer took on the onerous task of giving each piece a mark. The forms with the highest average were declared the winners and the best examples were exhibited in the corridors.

The Singing Competition also involved everybody. All forms competed and, having chosen their own pianist and conductor, learnt a set song and perfected another from their repertoire under her baton.

During the extra rehearsals some form staff listened, encouraged and 'kept the peace!' Despite the occasional false start, or nervous hands scattering sheets of music, the performances before an outside judge were often lively and of a high standard, though some forms were merely thankful to have reached the end all together on the right note!

Fewer people took part in the Speech Competition, of course, but here again, all forms in English lessons chose their representatives to read set poems and dialogues. The competition certainly helped the English staff to choose girls to read in the annual Carol Service, and to act in the plays which were produced at this time.

The first play to be performed at Netherton Arts Centre was Mrs Gaskell's *Wives and Daughters*, a good choice for a girls' school, with Jill Speake playing the only important male part. It was exciting for the cast to be acting in a real theatre, and it led the way to other productions, including an amusing *The Happiest Days of Your Life*. Miss Chilton went on to tackle the more ambitious *As You Like It*, with Margaret Madin as a charming Rosalind, and later on came *A Midsummer Night's Dream*, *A Winter's Tale* and James Bridie's *Tobias and the Angel*.

There was now no longer any need, however, to find taller girls with gruff voices to play male parts. At last the Grammar School had arrived on the scene, though co-operation between the schools was very gradual. As Virginia Baker (Mrs Poole) recalls:

> *Whether by accident or design, few men entered our environment. We remained a feminine institution where trousers were rarely seen and never on a lady.*

Nevertheless, soon after the war finished, at a time when clubs flourished – Science, Choir, French, Geography – a Dance Club was formed to which the Sixth Form boys were invited. After the initial shyness had worn off, pupils of the Grammar School and the High School became good friends and towards the end of the season a dance was held, which was thoroughly enjoyed by all. Certainly, dancing with boys was more exciting than the constant K1, P1, of wartime.

A little later a joint Dramatic Society was formed and several play readings held. The two Sixth Forms combined and shared the local Baptist Chapel in Priory Road for their Higher School Certificate examinations. Some girls ventured over to St James's Road for Physics

'A Midsummer Night's Dream' 1958

Costume drawing by D. Tovey

lessons. Later still came Prefects' Parties, the Sixth Form Dance and, amazingly, the appointment of the first male member of the Staff, Mr Protheroe, to teach Physics. Miss Ambrose called him *'the bravest man in Dudley'* but the girls could not have frightened him too much, as he stayed until his retirement, long after the School became Comprehensive.

It was in music that co-operation was most enjoyed. Fathers, Grammar School Staff and boys turned themselves into very presentable sailors, Chinese gentlemen and peers of the realm for three excellent Gilbert and Sullivan productions of *HMS Pinafore, Iolanthe,* and *The Mikado.* Produced by Miss Crump, they were notable for the remarkable alto voices of Averil Tilley as Little Buttercup and the Fairy Queen, and Miss Woolgar (Mrs Bould) as Katisha. There was also an excellent choral performance of *Dido and Aeneas* at the Technical College.

**'HMS Pinafore'**

The two Schools also went 'together' on a day trip to Portsmouth, though strict segregation was enforced, with Sixth form boys at one end of the train and Sixth form girls at the other, and Staff on duty in the middle between First Year boys and girls. Even during the tours of the Maritime Museum and HMS Victory, care was taken that never the twain should meet!

*The Cornflowers* in the Fifties are full of accounts of various other expeditions as girls enjoyed the new freedom to travel after the war years. There were many theatre trips to Stratford and Birmingham, another to see Peggy Ashcroft in *Electra* at the Old Vic, youth hostelling with Miss Fleming and other members of the Geography Department at Dolgelly and in Yorkshire. For the younger girls, regular visits were made to Cadbury's, Wedgwood's, Jodrell Bank and many other places.

The School also began to look towards Europe. Very soon after the war an unusual link was made with Europe when a German programme in the Oversea Services was based at the School. A BBC reporter spent a week taping various lessons and savouring the School's daily routine. 'Assistantes' came over to perfect their English and help with the teaching of French and German. 1949 saw the restart of school expeditions abroad with a visit to the Loire, and in 1951 a party of Sixth Formers and six members of Staff sat bolt upright all night in Spartan third-class compartments on their way

**Trip to Dolgelly 1953**

**Trip to Palace of Westminster in London 1956**

to spend 12 days at Servos, a village situated at the foot of Mont Blanc. Miss Fisher recalls the *'walk to the Blue Lake'*:

**"***Trudging through deep snow our French guide kept saying 'ten minutes more' every twenty minutes. Eventually we arrived at the lake only to find it covered in snow, so quite invisible. The next day's walk was to a glacier which turned out to be closed for the winter!***"**

There followed skiing holidays at Zermatt, a trip to Bruges, and even more memorable, an Easter holiday expedition to Milan, Rome and Florence, led by Miss Hawes. It was exhilarating to walk round the Colosseum, the Baths of Caracalla, the ruins of Ostia, St Peter's and along the Appian Way, places only to be read about a few years earlier. The party was quite awestruck when they heard that

**Trip to Blois in France 1949**　　　　　　　　　　　　　**Visit to Italy 1956**

Miss Sarmiento had been granted an audience with the Pope, a little less so when they found that 9999 others were to be there! Florence was just as enjoyable, in spite of the convent being bitterly cold and the sheets damp! It was regarded as a triumph that not one of the party was mown down by Italian traffic.

Collections in aid of many charities remained a part of school life until the School closed. A monitress coaxed money out of pockets into little patterned bags on Tuesday morning, which was put towards a charity, chosen by each form only after heated debate at the first Form Council of every term.

When the Mayor of Dudley launched a fund in memory of Duncan Edwards, the famous Dudley-born young footballer killed in the Munich air disaster, every form, by means of beetle drives, a laundry service, car-cleaning and other ingenious ideas, raised money towards building a Youth Centre in the Priory Estate. Later, in 1960, World Refugee Year, the School was the largest single contributor to the Dudley total, and two pupils, Judith Allen and Gwyneth Davies, were chosen to attend the Finale in the Albert Hall. DGHS can be proud of the many donations it has made to less fortunate people.

**Presentation for Duncan Edwards Memorial Fund**

## THE STAFF ROOM

The Staff Room, particularly during the Fifties and Sixties, was a very happy place. This is perhaps surprising, considering that there were many strong characters there, and a fair sprinkling of eccentrics! There was, however, an intense loyalty, both to Miss Ambrose and the School, which bound them together. Old Girls will have their own memories of various members of Staff, but it has been possible here to write about only the most long-serving.

Miss O'Dwyer (1925-1959), or 'OD' as she was known to everyone, was an exceptional person. Near retirement, with her iron grey hair, tanned face and neat sweater and shorts, she was still a trim figure on the hockey-field and in the Gym/Hall (alas, no proper Gym!).

She revolutionised the teaching of gymnastics, doing away with old-style 'drill'. She believed that each pupil should exercise according to her own body rhythm. Apparatus was not there simply to enable girls to vault one after another; individuals and groups had to think what use could be made of it and enjoy a challenge. Many Old Girls can thank her for the self-control, poise and confidence she instilled in them.

She was also a woman of many parts. She spent her holidays painting in Iona and used her artistic talents in teaching 'Dudley writing'; she wrote the words of the School Song; a fluent speaker with high principles, she readily joined in School Council debates; and she took charge of Sex Education, a subject in which the School was a pioneer. She had a good sense of humour, and it was in one of these lessons that she admitted being 'stumped' for the only time in her career. One 11-year old, having listened to OD's carefully prepared talk on the facts of life, exclaimed contemptuously, 'Well, I can't see anything in it!'

Miss Chilton (1930-1960) was also a versatile member of Staff. Tall, angular, with bushy hair and an aristocratic tilt of the head, she came to teach the Kindergarten children, to whom she showed affection and inexhaustible patience, and stayed to teach younger girls in the main School.

She had very individual methods of dealing with children. No other member of staff would dare to cry *'Cooo-eeee!'* in a high-pitched voice to quell a hubbub, but uttered by her it was effective, and her pupils accepted and respected her eccentricities.

She taught English and History, and could turn her hand to any form of arts and crafts, using nimble fingers to produce wonderful headdresses, crowns and puppets. But it was in Oral English that she achieved most. She insisted on clear speech and, with a natural feeling for drama and verse, she took over the production of many school plays with outstanding success. So meticulous was she that even the hems of costumes had to be sewn in the right shade!

When Miss Sarmiento (1942-1973) left the School after 31 years, Miss Richards wrote in *The Cornflower*:

❝*'We have a charming lady come to teach Spanish and French'. That was Miss Sarmiento as first described to me many years ago; and the 'charming lady' stayed in Dudley, revolutionising the French Department and thereby bringing fame and pride to the School.*

*Miss Sarmiento's consuming interest was in devising new and better ways of teaching Modern Languages; she was, indeed, one of the early advocates of greater oral work, and based all her lessons on a rigorous but adaptable system of questions and answers. How her voice resounded down the corridors; how her gifts for drawing and play-acting drew a response from even the poorest linguist; how college and university sent their students to watch her dynamic lessons; and how her former pupils returned again and again to thank her and to recall old times!*

*A vivid personality, sometimes tenacious to the point of obstinacy, courageous, quickly moved to laughter (and exasperation!), that was 'the charming lady'.*"

Miss Clifford (1942-1968) came to teach English in 1942 and, as well as becoming Head of Department and, for three years, Second Mistress, she managed the Library, edited *The Cornflower*, inspired a Literary Society and did countless tasks as an assistant producer of plays, usually behind the scenes. She had a great knowledge and love of literature and expected high standards from her pupils. Some called her 'a hard marker' and it is true that she was a stern critic of shoddy work. Her praise, however, could be generous and was doubly rewarding.

One of her passions was School Council and the support of individual liberty. She was much more ardent in promoting the cause of freedom than many who were to profit from it.

Many will remember her tripping lightly on her toes along the corridors, and she was still prepared to wield a hockey stick in the Staff team when most would have retired to the sidelines. Her colleagues will remember what fun she was. She had a wonderful sense of the ridiculous and would dissolve into helpless giggles on more pompous occasions!

An Old Girl, Rosemary Johnson, has written her memories of Miss Edwards (1949-1982):

"*Miss Edwards taught English for many years before taking over from Miss Clifford as Head of Department. When she retired the School had become a comprehensive, but the quality of her contribution to the life of the School – academic and otherwise – remained constant and former pupils still say how vividly they remember her lessons.*

*These lessons, often punctuated by peals of laughter, were always conducted with good humour and were something to be enjoyed. She brought to life our set texts, plays were read aloud and acted (by Miss Edwards, as well as by us); the complicated characters of 'Wuthering Heights' were defined by a family tree, and the English Language got its own family tree too. She had a knack of hitting on a simple thing that fixed the subject for ever in your mind. Even lessons on the semi-colon had a lasting effect on the style of one pupil! No wonder that her 'O' and 'A' level results were excellent.*

*She never wavered in her willingness to take on out-of-school activities and she was always available to answer the peculiar questions of little girls, helping us to see the background and wider context. She was also a sympathetic form teacher to all ages from First to Sixth Forms.*

*We know we were lucky to have Hilary Edwards as a teacher, and we still know!* "

Miss Hawes (1952-1982) taught Latin to pupils from the Second Year upwards, and also introduced a keen group to the delights of ancient Greek. She was an enthusiastic supporter of the West Midlands Classics Club, set up by her predecessor, Miss Hewison, which flourished into the 1980's. Miss Hawes could often be seen with a cohort of girls en route after school to Rowley Regis, Stourbridge, Bilston or Wolverhampton. Meetings were very varied and included play-readings, talks by eminent classical scholars, visits to Roman sites and occasional *'noctes festivae'* with Roman banquets – reclining on the floor!

She organised visits to Italy and, to enhance her own knowledge, she went on a Hellenic cruise, taking in twenty-two classical sites. This gave her a depth of understanding of the classical world which proved invaluable in her teaching of Classical Studies to 'O' level and 'A' level.

In a new departure, Miss Hawes also took on the provision of careers information for the School. As well as building up a library of prospectuses, she put girls in touch with employers, arranged visits to places of work and encouraged contact with local careers advisors. A major undertaking was the provision of weeks of work experience.

An Old Girl, Margaret Dews remembers Miss Hawes's genuine concern for pupils' welfare, her gentle yet firm manner and her love for her subject, which earned her a respect and affection which are still evident in the many Old Girls who come across her today in various local activities.

**Miss Bate**

Although not an inhabitant of the Staff Room, Miss Bate (1934-1963), School Secretary for 29 years, was a corner-stone of the School. Hers was the first face to be seen by visitors, and her pink cheeks and warm smile made everyone feel welcome.

She worked in a room, rather than an office. No computers, not even a photocopier, of course – only a battered typewriter and a series of assistants whom she trained, and who regarded her with the affection usually reserved for a favourite aunt. Her desk was littered with papers, but she was very efficient and could always find the right one. Often she went home late; it was unthinkable that she could leave work unfinished. She never seemed to mind the constant interruptions of staff begging for an examination paper to be typed or children feeling sick. She was, indeed, everyone's friend.

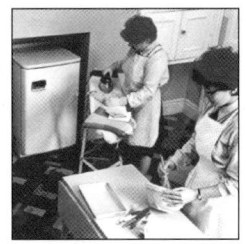

## Section Six

# The Sixties

ANYONE APPROACHING THE SCHOOL and reading the words on the Foundation Stone knew that October 1960 was to be an important date in the life of the School as it was exactly 50 years since the new building was occupied, and plans for a celebration were laid well in advance:

*"These were to consist of an Open Day for parents, and a service to be held on the morning of 21st October at St Thomas's Church, followed in the afternoon by a special celebration in the School Hall. We were greatly honoured to learn that the Bishop of Worcester would be speaking to us at the service, and that a special 'Te Deum' was being composed for the occasion by Dr Percy Young.*

*During the succeeding weeks Miss Crump worked hard to teach us the music straight from the production line, so to speak, one section being learnt while the next was being written, and, though nothing similar had been attempted before, the School rose to the challenge admirably and seemed to enjoy both the practices and the actual performance.*

*The Open Day for parents was held in the afternoon and evening on the day before the main celebration. Many form rooms contained displays of work, ranging from an exhibition of Roman Britain to a mouth-watering array of delicacies concocted by the Domestic Science students. This was interesting not only for the parents but for the girls too and, walking around the corridors during the dinner hour, one could hear 'oohs' and 'ahs' of pleasure as*

**Girls entering St Thomas' Church**

*half-forgotten First Form efforts were discovered hanging on the Studio walls, or a mother or aunt picked out in strange-looking antiquated gym tunic on the old school photograph.*

*At the Commemoration Service, the Bishop reminded us of the history of the School. The 'Te Deum' was sung and was accompanied on the organ by Mr Frank Edwards. Later, the Bishop and several other guests returned to have lunch at the School.*

*In the afternoon the final stages of the celebrations began with very interesting and amusing talks given by two former High School girls, Miss Hilda Foley and Miss Doreen Burton. Everyone enjoyed listening to their lively descriptions of school life as they knew it, the kindergarten, the knee-length gym tunics, the long, black stockings, and the shock the School received when one daring mistress had her hair cut into the new bob. These light-hearted anecdotes served to make us realise that, though fashions may change over the years, the schoolgirl is very much the same now as then, and forged a real link between the School past and present.*

*After this came the part which appealed most to the girls. The celebration cakes, specially baked and beautifully decorated by the Domestic Science students were eaten, and a toast drunk to the School – in lemonade!* "

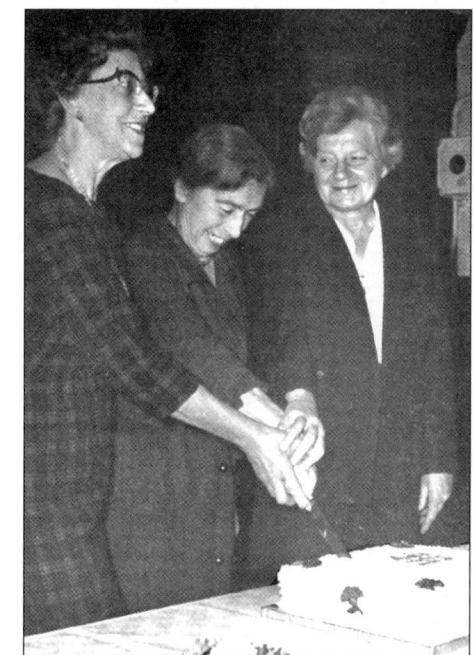

**Miss Ambrose cutting the Jubilee Cake**

DUDLEY HIGH SCHOOL
OLD GIRLS' ASSOCIATION

JUBILEE DINNER
1910 - 1960

SATURDAY, 3rd DECEMBER, 1960
AT THE
STATION HOTEL   -   DUDLEY

*President:*
Miss M. B. AMBROSE

*Chairman:*
Miss MARGERY H. OSBORN

At the Old Girls' Jubilee Dinner, which was held later in December, each decade since 1910 was recalled by an Old Girl of the period.

The decade of the Fifties was represented by one of the School's most renowned ex-pupils, Jennifer Smith, now Dr Jenny Tonge, who attended DGHS from 1951-1958. After she qualified as a doctor at University College, London, Jenny went into general practice and community health, specialising in

**Guest Speakers at the Jubilee Dinner 1960**

*Mrs Gilbert Griffiths (Bertha V Gill 1909-1920), wife of the Recorder of Dudley.*

*Mrs Little JP (Dorothy Round 1915-1927)*

*Mrs Saunders (Brenda Brookes 1927-1934), a solicitor to the Supreme Court.*

*Mrs Shaddock (Eileen Watson 1939-1959), wife of an Army officer.*

*Dr Jenny Tonge MP (Jennifer Smith 1951-1959).*

family planning and gynaecology. She also pursued her love of local politics, becoming a borough councillor in Richmond-on-Thames. In 1997, she was elected as a Liberal Democrat MP for Richmond-on-Thames and was re-elected in 2001. She has appeared on BBC's *Question Time* and is now the Liberal Democrat spokesperson for Overseas' Development.

Jenny has paid tribute to the training she received at DGHS as School Council Secretary for two years, revising the School Constitution and getting it through School Council. This has served her in good stead in her political life.

**Jennifer Tonge MP**

**Ashleigh**

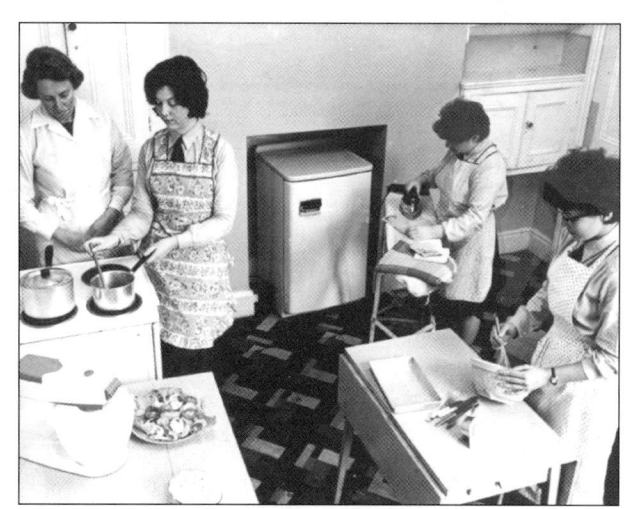

**Domestic Science Room in Ashleigh**

There were other causes for celebration in the early sixties. In 1960, Ashleigh, a house in Ednam Road, was bought by the Education Authority and the ground floor became part of the School. It comprised a large Music Room and a set of rooms for the teaching of Housecraft. The kitchens were equipped with all the latest labour-saving devices, a washing machine, spin-drier, food mixer, refrigerator and electric and gas cookers. As *The Evening Dispatch* wrote at the time, *'It will help them to become better housewives!'* Adjoining was a small but fully-furnished dining room, where meals could be served to fortunate guests. The official opening took place in May 1961 when parents of the Housecraft class were entertained to tea.

There was even more to celebrate the following year. Throughout her time in school, Miss O'Dwyer had an over-riding ambition to have a purpose-built Gymnasium. Since 1910, the Hall and Gym had been one and the same. Sadly, Miss O'Dwyer was never to see her ambition realised, but in December 1962 the Gym, built to face down the South Border, became a reality – after a 30 year wait.

Two years later, the School enthusiastically joined in the celebration of Shakespeare's Quatercentenary. Over many years, parties of girls had visited the Royal Shakespeare Theatre and enjoyed productions there. Now a Shakespeare Scrapbook Competition and a Shakespeare Quiz were held, and the songs chosen for the Singing Competition were settings of Shakespeare's words. Scenes from *A Midsummer Night's Dream* were performed in the garden and there was a remarkable production of

**'A Winter's Tale'**

*A Winter's Tale* at the Netherton Arts Centre. Of those who saw it or took part in it, who can forget the verse so beautifully spoken by Ann Bagnall and Susan Lawley in the leading roles, or Rosemary Johnson as a magnificent Paulina?

Special mention must be made of Sue Lawley OBE, who has become perhaps the most famous Old Girl. Having studied Modern Languages at Bristol University she joined the *Western Mail and Echo* in Cardiff as a graduate trainee and from there moved to BBC Plymouth as a sub-editor, reporter and presenter. In 1972 she became one of the main presenters of the BBC's early evening current affairs programme, *Nationwide*. Since then she has made her name as an interviewer, newscaster and chat show host – presenting the *Six o'clock News*, *Nine o'clock News*, *Wogan* and *Question Time*. She has also presented General Election, Budget and other popular current affairs programmes, such as *Here and Now* and *The Crime Squad*. Since the late 1980's she has been the custodian of BBC Radio Four's *Desert Island Discs* where, most weeks, she casts away the great and the good, together with eight of their favourite pieces of music. Sue left the School in 1964 – a momentous year of 'goodbyes'.

Sue Lawley in 'Nationwide'

Mr and Mrs Bradney retired as caretakers after 30 years' service. They were succeeded by Jack and Joan Westwood who stayed on as joint caretakers to the Dudley School. Liked by everybody, it would be difficult to imagine two more friendly people. 1964 was also the year of Miss Ambrose's retirement. Not long before she retired, Miss Ambrose had some kind words to say about the School:

Mr and Mrs Bradney

"*Whatever the School was engaged in, collecting for post-war charities, organising a revolt against stockings, or merely arguing, it seems to have done it with all its might. I have myself no doubt that behind all this sense of 'commitment' was the driving force of Miss Frood, with her passionate love of freedom, her faith in youth, and her delight in taking risks. In her day Dudley became known far beyond the Midlands, partly because of the experiments in school government, of which she was an excellent pioneer, and partly also because of the flair she showed in discovering and encouraging the genius of Marion Richardson, whose new approach to art is part of educational history. The same intuition made Dudley High School one of the first few in the country to teach Modern Dance.*

*But whatever has changed, some things are constant. The School is still alive and spirited: while it is true that our best friends would hesitate to call us quiet, or meticulously tidy, I believe we have been singularly fortunate in attracting, during our fifty years, a wonderful succession of teachers and other workers who have served the School with affection, devotion and skill. Sometimes bewildered, but never undaunted, they remained dedicated to their duties in 'official' working hours, and involved themselves week by week and with like enthusiasm in extra-mural activities, which modern programmes of education entail.*

*So all over the world today there are old DGHS girls who look back at their School as a place where they learned something of value, where they were happy and which they like to remember. We can look back to our past with affection and gratitude, and to the future with courage and confidence.*"

Miss Ambrose, of course, did not comment on the part she had played during her 23 years as Headmistress!

Miss Kellett (1964-1970), who arrived at the School in 1964, could not have been more different from Miss Ambrose. She was a large lady, with a jolly face and charming smile, and her footsteps could be heard pounding the corridors long before she arrived on the scene. She was kind and generous, but it was not always easy to gauge her mood on any particular day, and sparks sometimes flew unexpectedly. It was not surprising that some of the Sixth Form nicknamed her *Hurricane Freda!*

She was very concerned about high academic standards and the moral welfare of the pupils, but she never felt entirely happy with the role of School Council and its valuable committees, nervous perhaps of a system in which the pupils could easily outvote the staff had they wanted to. Over the years, however, she came to accept the system. In 1970, when she left to become a successful head of Birkenhead High School she introduced some of DGHS's ideas about self-government. She was later awarded an OBE for her services to education.

**Miss Kellett**

Although Miss Kellett was Head for only six years, those years were notable for a number of innovations. Perhaps one of the most successful ventures was Friday Club, a youth club where High School and Grammar School pupils could join in many activities, or simply meet and relax on Friday evenings. It proved so popular that it continued into the comprehensive era, later with an offshoot for junior pupils on Monday evenings. Many worked for the Duke of Edinburgh Award scheme and we were proud that Jennifer Aston became the first person in Dudley to be invited to Buckingham Palace for a gold award.

The highlight of the year was the Christmas dinner, cooked and served by members of the Club to a large number of Senior Citizens. There was also an entertainment, and the guests made it obvious on every occasion that they hoped for another invitation the following year.

During these years the School continued to raise large sums for various charities. With the less fortunate still in mind, over 200 girls and boys together with some of the staff took part in a 25 Mile Overnight Walk on behalf of the homeless, organised by Mr Patterson. The route took them round and through the Borough of Dudley. Disregarding the rain and wind, parents took up strategic positions to watch, encourage and refresh the walkers, but found most of them unwilling to pause on their journey in case they were unable to start again! Welcome refreshments were served at Halesowen Church Hall before the weary band faced the last '100 miles' through Brierley Hill to Dudley. As a result, a cheque for £1400 was presented to the Shelter Organisation.

The arts continued to flourish and once again the School combined with the Grammar School, this time in the production of a more modern musical, *Salad Days,* at Netherton Arts Centre. Perhaps more

**Preparing turkeys for Christmas – late 1960's**

**Presenting the proceeds of The Walk to Shelter.**

successful were three outstanding performances of *Culhwch and Olwen*. With music by William Mathias and words by Glyn Thomas, it was written for the 1967 National Eisteddfod and based on an old Welsh tale. Mr Lewis, the Musical Director of Dudley suggested that the School should give its English premiere and it was the first time that dancers had taken part.

Junior and Senior Choirs, instrumentalists (playing some very strange instruments!), the choral speech group and dancers all practised separately, only coming together a few days before the first performance, attended by Dr Mathias himself. He sat on the front row, with a broad smile on his face and said he was thrilled by such an unusual interpretation of his music.

The Senior Choir at this time was reaching a very high standard of performance under the baton of Miss Dean, and at the end of the 60's a tour of America became a possibility. After a lot of hard work

**Cleaning the Mayor's car for Oxfam**

**Car maintenance instruction for the Sixth Form**

and planning, and many problems and hitches which Miss Kellett helped to iron out, the choir left for America in the summer of 1970. The party was making the visit on an exchange scheme with girls from a school in Muskegon who had visited Dudley the previous summer.

The tour included New York, Washington, Niagara and other venues, where members of the party were guests of the schools and colleges at which they were to perform. They received letters from Mrs Richard Nixon and Mrs Dwight D Eisenhower, appreciating that the girls were helping to promote international understanding through music and dance.

Other pupils were also able to go abroad in an unusual way, for it was at this time that Dudley schools first experienced the educational cruises organised by British India. A fortnight on *SS Dunera*, *SS Nevasa* and *SS Uganda* enabled pupils, not only to visit such far-flung places as the Canary Islands,

**'Culhwch and Olwen'**

**School orchestra 1962**

Casablanca, Athens, Venice, the Holy Land and the Pyramids, but also to get a taste of boarding-school life in unusual circumstances. It meant overcoming home-sickness – and sea-sickness! – sleeping in dormitories, deciding on activities, boat drill, attending lessons and lectures, contributing to prize-winning log books, and joining in the fun of fancy dress parades, discos, and good company. The accompanying staff enjoyed themselves too, though being on duty virtually from 7.00am until 10.00pm and

**Girls on US tour 1970**

**Dance team – US tour 1970**

**'SS Dunera' cruise 1968 – sightseeing in Athens**

negotiating 70-odd stairs to the dormitories hardly made it the picnic that some people believed! On the first cruise on *SS Dunera* the party was delighted to find that the ship's doctor was Jill Speake, a former Head Girl.

Nearer home there was a feeling of spaciousness. The Prefects, who had earlier been squeezed into a small cubbyhole in the top corridor, had moved reluctantly into the Annexe. Now, with the rest of

## DUDLEY GIRLS' HIGH SCHOOL

### Excuse Book

N.B.—Regular and Punctual attendance is required.

Pupils must never be absent, except for health, or important business, without having first obtained permission from the Head Mistress.

Absence for "pleasure" is not permissible unless the circumstances are very exceptional.

**Foundations of new School Hall 1969**

**An aerial view of School – 1960's**

the Sixth Form, they found a new home on the first floor of Ashleigh. This provided two classrooms, and a comparatively luxurious Common Room, which boasted a carpet, window seats and armchairs.

In 1969 the Annexe at the rear of the old Hall was demolished and at last a new Hall was built. It provided excellent accommodation for assemblies, examinations, musical performances and dance. The old Hall became a new Library, with a more academic atmosphere. Later two mobile classrooms, M1 and M2, made their appearance.

Despite these improvements, ripples of anxiety were already affecting parents and staff, if not pupils. Terms such as 'Comprehensive', 'Sixth Form College', 'amalgamation' and 'co-education' were being bandied about and it was obvious that big changes were in the air.

But, as yet, surely no one had envisaged that, before long, the old buildings and the new would be flattened to make way for a municipal car park.

**The Staff 1959-1960**

## Section Seven

# The Seventies

WHEN MISS KELLETT LEFT AT CHRISTMAS 1970, she said that she would remember particularly the friendliness, the real desire to help others less fortunate, the willingness to try out new ideas and the ready sense of humour. The new Headmistress, Miss Beryl Fisher (1971-1975), was well aware of all these characteristics of the School, as she had been a member of the Staff for 20 years and Deputy Head for 12 years.

Having spent most of her teaching life under the leadership of Miss Ambrose, it was natural that Miss Fisher should revert to her way of doing things. It was a difficult time to take over, but she was calm yet energetic, approachable and efficient, and a wonderful organiser, who believed in getting to know all the girls as individuals. With Miss Fisher as Headmistress, the School enjoyed a settled routine.

**Miss Fisher** *Copyright County Express*

Not for long, however, as 1972 was the year of the Fuel Crisis. No-one imagined when the supply of fuel eventually ran out on 25th January that it would be eight weeks before the School returned to normal. It was fortunate that Ashleigh, M1 and the Hall could be heated, except during power cuts. The Fourths and Fifths were able to enjoy half-day sessions. The Lower Sixth was accommodated in Baylie's Hall in Tower Street and the Upper Sixth in even greater luxury in the Town Hall's Banqueting Hall. The staff hurried from one to another during a particularly rainy period, and hastened through corridors at 36°F back to a chilly Staff Room.

Meanwhile the Junior Forms were given enormous projects to do at home and visited School now and again for new instructions, checking of work, Gym Club and Netball Tournaments.

At first the younger girls were thrilled to have days off school, but when they found how long they had to spend poring over encyclopaedias in the Reference Library, and how much written work was expected, they were glad when the School re-opened on 13th March.

*"My 'holiday' spoilt me. For, when it was over, I couldn't settle down. I think the strike was plain stupid – if this happens again next year I shall complain to the government."*

There was more fun in the summer of 1973 when it was decided that, for a change, the School should raise some money for itself and purchase a mini-bus. The biggest event was a Gala, which fortunately could be held on the field, as a showery morning turned sunny just in time. Every form provided a stall or a sideshow, and the School was proud to welcome the Worcestershire and England cricketers, Norman Gifford and Basil D'Oliviera, who came to lend their support and sign innumerable autographs. A particularly popular attraction was a football competition, when people attempted to shoot goals past Jim Cumbes, the Aston Villa goalkeeper. Altogether over £600 was raised.

**Prize winners – 1970's**

Later, a competition was organised to 'Guess the total weight of the Staff'. They were weighed all together on the public weighbridge and the total put in a sealed envelope. Individual weights were not revealed but the total seemed surprisingly large!

The School decided to perform *Noyes Fludde* as its last production to hail the end of an era. It wanted to involve as many people as possible to bring out the best in the more talented musicians. Besides singers, instrumentalists and dancers, an army of people was needed for making masks, scenery and costumes, for stage management, lighting, amplification, make-up, business management and refreshments.

Rehearsals began in March for soloists and instrumentalists, and in the Summer term for the strings, recorders and percussion, 'gossips' and animals. The work became more worthwhile and enjoyable when the different groups began to rehearse together. Progress had to be made early on, because the Hall was needed for external examinations throughout June. The 12 days from the end of examinations to the Dress Rehearsal included a Sports Afternoon, a visit to the Llangollen Eisteddfod as well as many other visits, so life was very hectic.

**Norman Gifford and Jim Cumbes at Gala**

**Handing over the minibus keys – 1974**

County Borough of Dudley
*Cleansing & Transport Department*
**LISTER ROAD, DUDLEY**                                   WEIGHPRINTER

| WEIGHT | TONS | DAY & MONTH | CODES | |
|---|---|---|---|---|
| GROSS | 2 · 12 | | | 43 cwts 3 qts. 2 lbs 13½ oz. |
| TARE | | | | |
| NETT | | | | |

**Staff at the weighbridge 1973**

Order began to come out of chaos, and the first performance took place in front of a full house, despite a literal flood outside. The drama was increased by the presence of dancers, representing waves in the storm scene. What helped most of all were the lively appreciative audiences, who joined in the singing of the hymns. This was an enjoyable and memorable production of which the School could be justly proud, and which was a highlight of the last few days of the School's existence.

Among the girls who were pupils during the last years of the School, two deserve special mention:

**Jenny Wilkes**

Jenny Wilkes, who gained a degree in Communication Studies at Coventry, started broadcasting on Dudley Hospital Radio and BRMB in Birmingham. She later moved to BBC Radio WM at Pebble Mill and has since become a very familiar voice throughout the Midlands. She has also presented television programmes for *Midlands Today* and hosted a BBC exhibition at Gas Hall, Birmingham.

Helen Pitchford, who left the School in 1974, studied at Liverpool. She and Andy Wilkins, her husband, a geo-technical engineer, became Christian missionaries in Nepal. They were allowed into the country only if they could help the indigenous people to learn skills for themselves, and Helen literally saved a baby from starvation. Tragically, when they and their three children were returning to Nepal for a second spell, the plane crashed into a mountain, with the loss of all on board.

The Pitchford and Wilkins Memorial Trust has been set up to provide opportunities for the poor and destitute, and money has been made available to train engineers at English universities to work in Nepal.

## Section Eight
# The End of the High School

THE FIRST SUGGESTION that the Dudley Education Authority intended to change the status of Dudley Girls' High School came as early as 1966. A plan was put forward to amalgamate the Grammar School with the High School. This was amended two years later, making the Grammar School into a Sixth Form College.

Anne Emery, the Editor of *The Cornflower* commented:

> "'Sixth Form College', 'Comprehensive', 'amalgamation'; these three phrases have periodically been buzzing around for the past year. Shock, I think, was the first feeling of most of the girls, when they heard that Dudley Girls' High School was to cease to exist. I could not believe the headlines in the daily newspaper, which stated that we were to become part of a Sixth Form College. After trudging backwards and forwards in all weathers for six years, I had complacently taken it for granted that the School would go on for ever. With its long history, of which it is proud, the date of its founding seems almost as far back as the Conquest. Dudley without the High School seems like December without Christmas – impossible. Yet the same was thought of London Bridge – which is now boosting the tourist trade of America.
>
> The girls, however, quickly became used to the idea of change and many contemplated a Sixth Form College with delight, but our elders did not seem able to agree."

**Tree planting in 1973**

It was true that the majority of Staff and parents disliked this plan, but opposition to it was as nothing compared with reaction to a third plan, which was put forward in 1971. In this, the Grammar and High Schools were to amalgamate with the Blue Coat School as a comprehensive, and DGHS would virtually cease to exist. The Home and School Association immediately launched a campaign. This culminated in a protest march to the Council Chamber, where a petition was presented. A meeting was arranged so that the Director of Education could explain the plan to parents and hear their response. The campaign was temporarily successful and plans were shelved for the moment.

However, it was obvious, even to junior pupils, that change would come. The Editor of *The Cornflower* decided to ask them what they understood and felt about local education plans. Their answers were often knowledgeable and thoughtful, but some were both remarkable and entertaining (see page 130).

Within the next two years, yet another plan was being discussed. This plan combined the two Schools with Park Boys' and Park Girls' Schools, and seemed likely to be passed by the Authority.

It was not a very happy time for anyone connected with the School. Meetings, when the Staff of all four Schools began to discuss the huge problems involved, were always

**Home & School Association petition**

*Who decides education plans in a town like Dudley?*
The Conservatives and the Labourers.

*What is a College of Education?*
A place where you are learnt to be a teacher.

*What is a University?*
(a) A place where you learn only one thing.
(b) A place where you are sent if you fail your 'O' Levels.

*What is a co-educational school?*
A school where there is no fixed timetable.

*What is meant by 'going comprehensive'?*
(a) Some schools are being demoralised
(b) Everybody from every school is going to another school.
(c) Everybody is going to be mixed up. The teachers are going to be mixed up too.

*Are you glad or sorry to be 'going comprehensive'?*
I am glad because:
(a) We shan't know the tops from the bottoms.
(b) We can swim with the boys.
(c) It saves us from splitting.
(d) It stops other people being jelus of us.
I am sorry because:
I think it is too much fuss and bother over nothing and I have had enough of muddy footballs being kicked in my face.

# AMALGAMATION?
DEIRDRE HOLDEN, V2.

**DUDLEY GIRLS' HIGH SCHOOL**

*FINAL DISTRIBUTION OF CERTIFICATES AND PRIZES*

by

The Rt. Rev. M. Mann

19th NOVEMBER, 1975

AT 7.15 P.M

---

ORDER OF PROCEDURE

School Hymn

The Chairman
    Mrs. D. Chambers

Headmistress's Report
    Miss. B. M. Fisher

Address
    by
    The Right Rev. M. Mann
    Bishop of Dudley

Distribution of Certificates and Prizes

Vote of Thanks
    by
    The Head Girl, Louise Popplewell

Violin Solo
    by
    Margaret Wilkinson
    Part of Sonata in G. Opus 13.   *Grieg.*

The National Anthem

amicable and constructive. But frustration and some bitterness was felt, no doubt by all four groups, as they saw the ethos of their own particular School being eroded by amalgamation. Some extraordinarily insensitive things were said and done. DGHS was supposed to be reassured when the Education Authority stated that it would be *slotted in* and, on one occasion, a Headmaster of a completely different school arrived uninvited and looked round the School, so certain was he that he and his pupils were taking over the building.

In 1974 the plan became a reality. The four Schools were to amalgamate but for a year to continue on four sites. Mr Austin of the Grammar School was appointed Headmaster, the Staff were assigned to new posts, the Sixth Form was to be divided between Grammar School and High School buildings, and Fourth and Fifth year girls, apprehensive but a little excited, were to be transferred to St James's Road. The following September, six forms of mixed 12-year-old pupils would be welcomed into the new Comprehensive. And so it came to pass.

In the last edition of *The Cornflower*, Mrs Doris Chambers, who had been a stalwart supporter of the School as a Chairman of the Governors for 10 years and a Governor for 20 years, said farewell:

*"I have experienced great joy in the pride and poise of the girls who have earned and spread the good record of the School, not only in this Borough and in our country, but in lands far overseas, where they have also served with success and distinction. Now we are on the brink of changes, and I am sure that the Governors share the apprehensions which the problems of those changes bring. We trust that the future can build upon the worthily established foundations of all these years of educational experience and progress.*

*As Chairman, I wish to thank all Governors who have served so loyally – and may I, on behalf of all of us, offer our sincere wishes for the continuance of high standards of approach and of achievement in the future. In surrendering its name, I am sure that DGHS will never lose its reputation.* **"**

## VIEWS OF SCHOOL LIFE

*First day: timid, feeling tiny,
Leather satchel hard and shiny,
Pristine blouse of cornflower blue,
Matching pair of hair slides too.
Pretty these, but Miss O'Dwyer
Sent me off posthaste to buy a
New and mousey-brownish pair;
Slides, she said, must match your hair!*

*If one hoped to make the grade
Rules just had be to be obeyed.
Keep well left upon the stairs!
Silence on the way to prayers!
At the end of every day
Put your indoor shoes away!
This the rule whose contravention
Brought my first (and last) detention.*

*Lessons started – new, exciting:
Physics, French and 'Dudley Writing'.
Often Miss O'D would get us
Making patterns out of letters,
Taking care with shape and form;
Loops were out, clean lines the norm.
No more backward sloping scrawl,
A new bold script prescribed for all.*

*Then came 'Speech', Miss Chilton's class,
Enunciation taught en masse:
"Five plump peas in pea-pod pressed…
Now girls, repeat!" We acquiesced
But giggled at her anguished howls,
Brought on by charmless Dudley vowels.*

*For me, though, nothing could compare*
*With English Grammar, lessons where*
*By using logic and deduction*
*We'd parse some complex clause construction.*
*Verbs and nouns and mood and tense...*
*Language at last made total sense.*
*The joy of words Miss Ambrose knew*
*From then on was my passion too.*

*The major black spots in my week*
*Were gym and games. Dressed like some Greek*
*On netball courts I'd dither, frozen,*
*Always the last one to be chosen.*
*Verrucas, though, when kindly shared,*
*Would guarantee one's being spared*
*From dancing in the Dining Hall;*
*Here dust and splinters welcomed all*
*Who tripped about with feet unshod*
*Where lunchers (and their shoes!) had trod.*

*But even worse than dance and gym*
*Were doomed attempts to learn to swim.*
*Clad in my gloomy gaberdine*
*I'd drag myself to Blowers Green*
*And Dudley Baths, so dank and chill*
*Their chlorine coldness haunts me still.*

*The terms sped by – as each one closed*
*A cleansing ritual was imposed*
*On every form; desks must be cleaned*
*Till every nook and cranny gleamed.*
*A spotless inkwell was the aim,*
*So when Miss Sarmiento came*
*To check them out, no trace of blue*
*Would leave its smudgy residue.*

*We 'owned' our school; we cared about*
*The way it looked, inside and out.*
*The toilets just below N2*
*Were drab and nondescript in hue*
*Until one day the painters chose*
*To decorate in deepest rose.*
*Ablutions then, to our delight,*
*Became "apinktions" overnight!*

*Everything's gone now – desks and Hall,*
*Studio, staff room, labs and all*
*Our classrooms; just a memory*
*Are 1S2 and 1N3.*
*The netball courts I dithered on*
*Are rubble now. All trace has gone*
*Of Miss Frood's garden – nothing left.*
*Playing fields too, forlorn, bereft,*
*Await their soulless destiny,*
*The advent of the JCB.*

*Three hundred homes, they say, are planned*
*By those developing the land.*
*Maybe we'll see an Ambrose Drive*
*To keep school memories alive...*
*Whatever names, though, planners choose,*
*Old Girls like me will never lose*
*Affection for those days we knew*
*When hair-slides never could be blue!*

*(Margaret Dews – 1955-1962)*

The last word belongs to Miss Fisher:

"The last few years have been amongst the most uncertain in the history of the School in that the future has been symbolised by a question mark. Yet, in spite of this, we have maintained our academic standards and involved ourselves in as many activities. This has been possible because in true DGHS tradition the Staff have maintained the friendly team spirit and have been prepared to give and not to count the cost. The Dudley School must be built on the traditions of four Schools and must emerge as a School with its own individuality. But I am sure that, on one of the cornerstones, will be inscribed Dudley Girls' High School."

## Section Nine

# School Uniform

THE FREQUENT REFERENCES TO SCHOOL UNIFORM in School Council minutes and *The Cornflower* reveal the interest shown in the subject. DGHS uniform changed during the years under the influence of fashion, lifestyles and wartime restrictions. To the casual reader many items may seem trivial but to the pupils of the day they were important topics to be discussed and voted upon.

Photographs of the early days show the styles of clothing in the late 19th century. In 1910, heavy duty gym tunics, two inches above the knees when kneeling, long-sleeved navy blouses, long black woollen stockings held up by suspenders attached to a liberty bodice, and heavy woollen knickers with cotton linings were the order of the day in winter. The summer uniform refers to the tunic having three pleats and a velvet top, worn with white delaine blouses and stiff straw hats.

**Circa 1880**

Old Girls recalled the changes made during the war years of 1914-18:

> *"...we came to School in almost anything we could procure in the shape of a hat, soft straws in summer and faded knitted caps in winter."*

It appears that the fabric used in blouses changed as well – to tussore and then blue cotton; and in style – to square necks, followed later by round collars. By the 1920's, when pupils were allowed some input into new designs, the tunic had become knee length and...

**About 1883**

> *...great skill and good suspender belts were required to ensure that no gap (known as a smile!) appeared between stockings and knickers during even the most vigorous gymnastic lessons.*

It is not surprising, that a little later, tunics and stockings were discarded for indoor PE lessons! Winter velour hats with hat bands were exchanged for berets and, in summer, panama hats, which...

> *...after a shower of rain would shrink and become permanently waved.*

The Uniform List for 1935 was:

### WINTER
*Velour brimmed hat with band and woven badge; overcoat (optional) navy; navy raincoat; navy tunic; light blue blouses with wide collars; money belt; knee-high socks, outdoor and indoor shoes; plimsolls; navy blue knickers with pocket (for handkerchief); Greek tunic for dancing; shoe bag; small hand towel; Cash's name tapes.*

### SUMMER
*Panama hat with band and badge; blazer with badge sewn on pocket; summer dresses.*

The constraints of clothing coupons in force from 1939-49 meant that uniform was maintained as far as possible and unwanted or outgrown

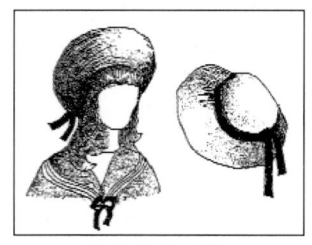

**1920's**

**1940's**

items were offered for sale through the School. Fashion played a significant part in influencing the rules in the late 1940's and the 1950's. In 1948-49 it was the 'new length' skirts that led to the introduction of pleated navy shorts as an alternative to the tunic for games. A few years later, it was agreed that hooped petticoats – the current fashion – were not practical with school uniform; for one thing they took up too much room when girls were sitting on the floor for assembly! This period saw the introduction of a regulation School scarf – not a football scarf! – and a compulsory School tie, which led to a change of blouse collar design. Cornflower blue cardigans and blazers made their appearance in the early 1950's, as did strap purses.

School Council was very busy with dress proposals in the 1950's including, for 1951: *'During the summer term socks are to be worn with all types of shoes except sandals, and high heels are not to be worn.'*

For 1953: *'Outdoor shoes, other than boots or sandals should be black or navy blue. Belts other than tunic belts may not be worn with school uniform.'*

For 1954: *'Upper Fourths upwards may wear skirts and alternative dancing tunics.'* Cardigans with collars were out and a proposal for metal badges on berets was defeated.

In 1955, shoes appeared on the agenda again when it was decided that: *'Low-heeled shoes not exceeding one and a quarter inches in height should be worn and indoor shoes should be black or navy blue.*' A suggestion, in 1958, that berets should be cornflower blue was defeated but cornflower blue stockings – very fashionable! – were, in 1958, acceptable.

Wearing hats to and from School – a rule that was difficult to enforce once pupils left the building – was made optional in 1963, except for formal occasions, provided that a badge was displayed on a blazer or scarf. The whole School voted in 1964 on the choice of material for summer dresses. By 1971, school uniform was optional for Sixth Formers but they were not allowed to wear trousers or *maxi skirts*. A final freedom from School regulations was granted when long hair no longer had to be tied back!

1950's     1950's – Upper Fourth     1950's – Greek tunic

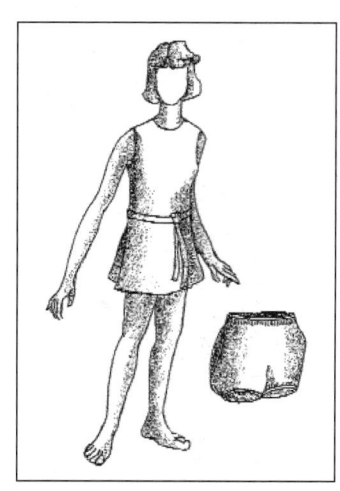

## Section Ten

# Careers A-Z

IN THE LIFETIME OF THE SCHOOL, the fortunes of women changed dramatically.

In the 1880's and 1890's it was unlikely that women would be admitted to Universities; they might – if they were lucky – become maidservants or governesses in large houses!

During the First World War, women started to be recruited to positions such as nurses with the Red Cross or ambulance drivers. By the 1920's, pupils had the opportunity of going to Universities and Colleges of Education. This trend continued into the 1930's but teaching posts were in short supply. All the women, whatever their status, had to resign on marriage. Therefore, all teachers were single. In the 1950's the situation changed and rules relaxed.

By 1941, unmarried women aged 18 to 30 were conscripted for National Service. They could be directed into the ATS, WRNS, WAAF or Women's Land Army, maybe into munitions factories or, as trainees, into nursing. In fact, they could be coerced into many roles previously held by men, unless they were already in reserved occupations. Equal pay, however, did not come until many years after the war had ended.

In the 1950's and 1960's, Dudley Girls' High School was sending 30-40 students each year to Training Colleges. As a result most Dudley schools employed former pupils as teachers.

A century on, the breadth of occupations in which the girls have become involved is enormous. Some of the careers taken up by Dudley Old Girls are shown in the following list.

## CAREERS ALPHABET

**A** Accountant, Advertising, Air Traffic Controller, Almoner, Anaesthetist, Auditor, Artist, ATS, Aromatherapist, Actuary.

**B** Banker, Beautician, Biologist, Blood Transfusion Technician.

**C** Cancer Research, Careers Officer, Chef, Caterer, Chiropodist, Computer Programmer, Customs and Excise Officer, Civil Servant, Clerk, Chartered Accountant.

**D** Dentist, Doctor, Dance Instructor, Dairy Instructor, Demonstrator, Dispenser, Dental Receptionist.

**E** Educational Administrator, Examiner, Estate Agent.

**F** Farmer, Forensic Scientist, Food Scientist, Furniture Design, Financier.

**G** General Practitioner, Government Adviser, Gymnastic Instructor, Governess, Governor.

**H** Health Visitor, Hotel Manager, Hotel Receptionist, Headmistress, Horticulturalist, Hairdresser, Hygienist.

**I** Income Tax Inspector, Information Centre Staff, Insurance Adviser, ICI Laboratory Technician, Inspector of Schools, Interpreter.

**J** Journalist.

**K** Kindergarten Teacher, Kennel Maid.

**L** Librarian, Lecturer, Local Government Officer, Linguist.

**M** Masseuse, Museum Staff, Missionary, Musician, Member of Parliament, Metallurgist, Midwife, Medical Photographer, Medical Researcher.

**N** Nurse, Nursery Nurse, Novice, Nun, News Editor (Newspapers).

**O** Open University Lecturer,
Occupational Therapist, Orthoptist,
Optician, Office Staff.

**P** Pharmacist, Policewoman,
Physiotherapist, Poultry Farmer,
Potter, Plotter (WRNS),
Pathology Technician, Publisher.

**Q** QARANC (Queen Alexandra's Royal Army Nursing Corps),
QARNNS (Queen Alexandra's Royal Navy Nursing Service).

**R** Radiographer, Reporter (News),
Riding Instructor, Radio Presenter.

**S** Surgeon, Speech Therapist, Solicitor,
Swimming Instructor, Store Manager,
Store Detective, Secretary, Social Worker,
Stage Manager, Scientist.

**T** Teacher, Tourism Officer,
Transport Police, Theatre Manager,
Teller, TV Presenter, Tennis Coach.

**U** University Administrator,
University Professor and Lecturer,
United Nations Personnel,
Underwriter.

**V** Voluntary Service Officer,
Voluntary Worker (various agencies),
Veterinary Nurse.

**W** WAAF, WRNS, Women's Land Army.

**X** X-Ray Technician.

**Y** Youth Worker,
Youth Employment Officer.

**Z** Zoo Keeper, Zoologist.